For the West Georgia Regional
Library

With a stringing of good wishes,
Kathryn Tucker Windham

November 3, 1988

A Serigamy of Stories

Kathryn Tucker and her brother Wilson dressed up to go to church

A Serigamy
of Stories

Kathryn Tucker Windham

A Muscadine Book

University Press of Mississippi
Jackson & London

Library of Congress Cataloging-in-Publication Data

Windham, Kathryn Tucker.
A Serigamy of stories.

1. Windham, Kathryn Tucker — Childhood and Youth.
2. Thomasville (Ala.) — Biography. 3. Thomasville
(Ala.) — Social life and customs. I. Title.
F334.T48W56 1988   976.1'245   [B]   88-5461
ISBN 0-86805-354-9 (alk. paper)

CONTENTS

Preface · 1

Our Front Porch · 3

Aunt Bet · 10

Piano Lessons · 25

Methodists and Baptists · 29

My Parents · 40

Kodaks and Hill's Pasture · 62

Laps and Rocking Chairs · 72

Wilson · 77

Barber Shops · 82

Lyles Carter · 85

Miss Lillie · 90

Expression · 92

Illnesses · 96

Town Characters · 103

Trains, Circuses, and Tent Shows · 107

Christmas · 113

Depression Days · 119

For my grandson,
D A V I D   W I L S O N   W I N D H A M

PREFACE

SERIGAMY is not in any dictionary. It is a made-up word, a word used in my mother's family for several generations, for so long that nobody now remembers who concocted it.

Roughly, the word means a whole lot, a heap of, a right smart, a goodly number, as in, "There was a serigamy of folks at the wedding," or, "A serigamy of cars passed the house on their way to the ball field," or, "He didn't have much money, but he had a serigamy of friends."

My father knew a serigamy of stories. Everybody in my family did. So this book is a collection of stories I grew up hearing, of stories about people I knew in Thomasville, the small southwest Alabama town where I lived, and of stories about me.

The stories, I hope, reflect the freedom and security of Southern small town life in the 1920s and early 1930s.

Perhaps these remembrances of my childhood will underscore the closeness that came from knowing everybody in the community, the acceptance and enjoyment of neighbors just as they were, and the laughter and friendships that bound us all together.

Perhaps they will stir memories for a serigamy of stories of your own.

Our Front Porch

LIKE THE AGE RINGS in a tree trunk, the layers of cretonne covers on our porch pillows marked the passing years in our family. On a chilly late March morning, while Thurza was passing around another batch of her hot biscuits, Mother would gaze out the dining room window and announce, "It will soon be warm enough to sit out on the porch. I'd better cover the cushions." Nobody was ever sure what prompted that annual announcement but no member of the family ever questioned it.

So right after breakfast, Mother walked down the hill to town to select the material for the covers from the bolts of cloth in the piece goods department at Bedsole's Dry Goods Company ("Bedsole's Goods Are Good Goods"). Miss Jodie Jackson had clerked at Bedsole's since right after Moses, as people used to say, and she could remember what colors and designs Mother had bought for our cushion covers for the past dozen or so years—in proper sequence—and exactly how many yards she needed. Miss Jodie could remember everything.

Miss Jodie could also tie the prettiest tulle bows of anybody in town. We didn't have a florist in Thomasville, so when there was a death in the community, friends took flowers from their own yards to the home of the bereaved. They gathered bouquets of whatever was blooming and went to Bedsole's to get Miss Jodie to pick out the right color of tulle (pale pink and lavender were her favorites for funerals) and to tie the bow for them. When she finished, the home-grown flowers looked as artistic and professional as any arrangement from a city florist, Mother used to say.

Once when Mother was buying cretonne at Bedsole's, a woman

came to thank Miss Jodie for roses she had sent to the woman's mother's funeral.

"I'm glad you liked them," Miss Jodie replied. "I told Sister, though, it was a shame your mother didn't die two weeks earlier—our roses were so much prettier then."

Mother didn't laugh, just kept on looking at the cretonne, but she couldn't wait to get home and tell us about it.

Miss Jodie was also famous for her chicken pies. She made her pie in a deep dishpan, and between the flaky bottom and top crusts were big chunks of chicken, dumplings and rich gravy. Nothing else. Real chicken pie, made the proper way. At dinners-on-the-ground, family reunions, graveyard cleanings and such, everybody tried to get a helping of Miss Jodie's chicken pie.

There was one occasion when my brother Wilson, Cousin Earl and Russell Stutts, teen-age boys who certainly were better raised, slipped out of church while the preacher was delivering a homecoming sermon, stole Miss Jodie's chicken pie off the long pine table in the grove, ate every bite of it, and put the empty dishpan back on the table. The three of them were grown men before they ever admitted their wrongdoing. By then even Miss Jodie could laugh about it. I'm not sure what color our porch cushions were the summer that happened, but Miss Jodie likely knew.

Miss Jodie held the record for working for one store longer than anybody else in Thomasville ever did, and when she finally retired, hundreds and hundreds of her customers came to the party Bedsole's gave for her.

The only other person who might have broken Miss Jodie's employment record was Miss Lillian Adams, who clerked at Kimbrough's ("The Great General Store"). Miss Lillian had been clerking at Kimbrough's for goodness knows how many years when she went home to dinner one day and didn't come back to the store.

Along about two o'clock, Will Kimbrough got worried about her (she had never been late before), and he sent somebody up to Miss Lillian's house to see if anything bad had happened to her.

His emissary returned with the report that Miss Lillian was all right. Fine. She was sitting on her front porch rocking, he said. Just rocking. She had decided she didn't want to work any more. And she never did. So Miss Jodie's record remained unchallenged.

After Mother had decided on the cloth she wanted to buy, Miss Jodie flipped the bolt of material over and over with the grace of a juggler, until dozens of loose folds lay on the counter in front of her, waiting to be measured and cut.

Back home again, Mother assigned Thurza or me to find the cushions, while she threaded her New Home sewing machine. Those cushions usually spent the winter in a trunk in a plunder room at the end of the ell, a room spoken of as The Far Room. There were a good many trunks in The Far Room. Daddy used to say the only inheritances our relatives ever willed us were trunks and Bibles. We did have a gracious plenty, almost a serigamy, of both.

I wanted to rip the old covers off the cushions, rip away layer after layer all the way back to before I was born, but Mother wouldn't let me.

"Each new layer makes the cushion softer and thicker," she said as she cut and pinned and stitched.

Mother didn't finish her sewing all in one day—there were always interruptions—but the amazing thing was that the day she did finish was always sunny and warm, just right for sitting on the porch. Daddy called it the gallery.

Porch or gallery, it was, weather permitting, the gathering place for our family, the place many of our family stories were told.

Our house sat on the corner, halfway up the hill from the Southern Railroad. Between our house and the railroad was the lumber yard, a shipping point for pine logs, many of them more than one hundred feet long. From our porch I watched workmen skin those logs, covering the red clay ground with strips of bark (Thurza used that bark to start fires around the wash pots in her back yard), and saw teams of oxen pull the skinned logs to the loading ramps beside the railroad tracks. Daddy called the logs pilings and said they were being shipped to Mobile.

That lumber yard lured my playmates and me. We played

chase there, balancing with outstretched arms as we ran the lengths of the skinned poles, jumping from one log to the next, climbing to the tops of the tall stacks. We played hide and seek, and we straddled the limber ends of the logs, bouncing up and down, pretending we were cowboys, Tom Mix or Ken Maynard, astride fine horses.

The porch faced west toward the lumberyard. It stretched across the front of the house, turned at a right angle to run along the north side of the living room, and then made another sharp turn to the north along the ell where four rooms (three bedrooms and The Far Room) opened onto it. Nobody ever sat on the porch along the ell, but it was a fine place to ride tricycles and, later, to learn to skate.

Mother's freshly covered cushions went onto the seats of four big rocking chairs (always painted green, though the shades of green varied, no matter what colors the cushions were) and down the long slatted bench that stood against the wall.

On summer nights I, in my one-piece seersucker pajamas, stretched out on that bench and fell asleep as the voices of my family mingled in talk and laughter, and the katydids chirped their noisy complaints. ("If you go put your hand on the tree, they'll hush their fuss," Aunt Bet said.)

The fragrance of honeysuckle and late-blooming four-o'clocks was overpowered at intervals by the smell of tobacco as Daddy filled his pipe and puffed hard to get it going.

When I was an older child, wakeful in my bedroom and tormented by vague fears, the sound of Daddy knocking the ashes out of his pipe to refill and light it for a midnight smoke reassured and comforted me; my fears vanished and I slept.

Mosquitoes were a pesky nuisance on the porch, especially at night. "Shut your eyes," Mother would say. "I'm going to squirt the scoot-skeet." She pumped the handle of the metal spray gun vigorously, directing the mist into the corner, toward the roof, and around the chairs and bench, leaving our ankles damp with insecticide.

"Please don't kill my lightning bugs," I'd say. My night's catch glowed like tiny neon signs in a glass jar near my dirty bare feet.

Later, Mother would wash the bottoms of my feet with a wet rag as I lay, nearly asleep, on the edge of my bed.

Each spring when Mother placed the new cushions in the chairs, arranged them to suit her notion, and stood back to admire her work, she would say to me, "I believe they're the prettiest ones we've had in years. We mustn't let them get wet." Mother had a way of saying "we" when she meant "you". I understood.

It was my responsibility to gather up the cushions and take them inside when a clap of thunder announced the approach of a summer shower. Cushions safe, I returned to the porch and leaned the chairs against the wall so their seats wouldn't get wet.

Meanwhile, Mother hurried from room to room, pulling down the windows where rain might blow in. "See about the telephone," she would call to me, and I would take the receiver of our wall telephone off the hook and let it dangle from its brown cord. I'm still not sure why.

Every summer day, rain or shine, I was expected to put fresh flowers, usually plumes of crepe myrtle (it blooms one hundred and one days each year), or purple blossoms of althea (they always had ants), in the pair of terra-cotta wall vases that flanked the front door.

Our front porch-sitting was done in the mornings or after the sun had gone down. Despite the thick tangle of wisteria, honeysuckle and ivy vines that twisted over the bannisters, curled around the posts and climbed to the roof, the porch was hot on summer afternoons.

In the mornings, I played paper dolls by the hour on that front porch. Bessie Gray, Thurza's daughter and my beloved playmate, cut our paper dolls out of old copies of *The Delineator* and *The Pictorial Review*. Occasionally Miss Jodie gave me a discarded pattern book from Bedsole's. What a treasure!

We filed our paper dolls by age (there were often long discus-

sions as to whether a paper doll was nine years old or ten) between the pages of a magazine, beginning with babies and going
all the way up to mamas and papas. Everybody who played paper
dolls had such a file. A thick file was a status symbol.

Miss Jodie also saved out-dated patterns for my family to use as
toilet paper in our outdoor privy. Other families might use old
catalogues, or even newspapers, but we had soft tissue paper patterns, lots of them, thanks to Miss Jodie.

Actually, we never referred to the structure behind the honey-
suckle-covered lattice as a privy. I never even heard the word
until I was about ten years old and was visiting my older sister's
in-laws in Cuba, Alabama.

"Would you like to go to the privy?" one of my young host-
esses asked soon after my arrival. I didn't know what she was
talking about, but I certainly didn't want to miss anything, so I
quickly answered, "Yes!" I was disappointed when I found out
what it was. We called our outhouse the Q. Why, I do not know.
But always it was the Q.

We didn't have inside plumbing until I was twelve years old.
Until then, we drew water from the well on the back porch, and
we walked down the winding path, past the chinaberry tree
where my tree house was, and past the peach orchard, to the Q.
Even after we had running water, we kept our well and the Q.

Daddy had our first bathroom installed in a room built on our
back screened porch, but it didn't stay there long. Daddy said no
toilet should be inside a house, so he had the bathroom moved
down to the very end of the ell, where he had half The Far
Room partitioned off for the tub and commode. We never had a
lavatory.

Mother often came out on the front porch in the mornings to
shell peas or butterbeans, or to peel peaches or figs. Bessie Gray
and I, and whoever happened to be "in residence" at the time,
helped.

I was given the colored and speckled butterbeans to make
playlike cows. "I know the speckled and colored butterbeans are
good," Mother would say, "but I like to use just the white ones."

Maybe it was Bessie Gray who showed me how to make cows. All it took for a cow was seven short pieces of a broom straw: four pieces for legs, two for horns and one for a tail. I lined my herd of cows up on the porch bannister, and I dared the green lizards who darted about in the vines to bother them!

Other early morning rockers on the front porch were Aunt Bet and Auntie, a really old lady who came visiting from Eutaw every now and then, bringing with her a black satchel filled with medicines that had been prescribed for her through the years.

Auntie and Aunt Bet spent their time arguing over the identities of photographs in an old album.

"I know that's a Stockton child," Auntie would say. "Look at that nose."

"Looks more like one of the Longs," Aunt Bet would reply. "Too much hair for a Stockton."

On the disagreement would go until they would decide the children in the photograph must be "Little Willie and Cousin Eugenia." All "unknown" photographs in our family are now called Little Willie and Cousin Eugenia.

The efforts to identify the pictures were always cut short because Aunt Bet had to leave to open the Post Office.

Aunt Bet

AUNT BET was, for some forty years, the postmaster (she scorned the use of the word "postmistress," considering it somehow insulting) in Thomasville, just as my grandmother, Harriett Newel Underwood Tabb, had been before her, and as her daughter, my cousin Tabb, was after Aunt Bet retired. Aunt Bet, though her salary was small, had a steady income when other members of the family lacked that security.

She had an unusual metal pin tray on her desk in the Post Office: the figure of a girl, possibly a dancer, holding out her full, stiff skirt. In that skirt, among the pins and paper clips, I often found the nickel that bought an after-school ice cream cone, or a Coca-Cola with a twist of lime (so sophisticated!) at Peoples Drug Store, or the dime that paid admission to the Saturday afternoon picture show. Except for my hurried "Thank you, Aunt Bet," we never mentioned our financial dealings, but Aunt Bet's nickels and dimes were the nearest thing I had to an allowance when I was a child.

"Miss Bettie got big ears," Thurza, our cook, used to say. "Means she a giving person. Big ears. Watch out for folks with little bitty ears—they stingy."

Aunt Bet's ears were big.

Living in a time when most people paid cash for what they bought, long before the day of plastic charge cards, she would often lend a customer the few dollars needed to pay for a C.O.D. package, to buy a new dress or suit for graduation, or to help purchase shoes and books for school. Each December she came to the aid of many financially strapped Santa Clauses.

She seldom kept records of such loans. "They'll pay me back

when they can," she'd say. Some members of the family, (ones with smaller ears) called her generosity foolish, impractical. She called it casting her bread upon the waters.

Aunt Bet likely inherited her generosity from her mother, Harriet Newel Underwood Tabb, the grandmother I never knew. The obituary written at her death in 1916 could have been written for Aunt Bet:

> For a quarter of a century, Mrs. Tabb served the people of Thomasville in the capacity of Postmaster, and during those years her many acts of kindness and words of praise helped the needy and encouraged the weak. The goodness of her friends she would magnify and their shortcomings she buried in the dark recesses of forgetfulness.

I wish I had known my Grandmother Tabb. "Mamá," the older grandchildren called her.

I heard stories about her, about how, as a young lady, she learned to paint still-life scenes and to play the harp at Marion Female Seminary.

Later, after her marriage in 1857, at age twenty, to Edward Tabb, there wasn't time for painting or for music. The couple moved to Waverly, Texas, where, during the war years, Grandfather served as a lieutenant in the Confederate militia, enlisting in Anderson, Texas.

With Grandfather away, Grandmother Tabb ran the plantation, riding out on horseback (side-saddle) each day to oversee the work of the slaves. And at night the carriage driver slept on a pallet outside her bedroom door to protect her and the children, just as he had promised his master he would do—the oft-told story of the faithful slave.

These war years were tragic for Grandmother Tabb: her two little children, five-year-old William Edward and twenty-month-old Carrie Cole, died within a few months of each other.

And the Yankees came. They piled up all her cotton in the front yard and set it afire. She stood on the porch and watched it burn, not saying a word.

Grandfather Tabb never adjusted to life in the post-war world.

He was, as they say, a good man but just never amounted to much. Of course, nobody in our family ever said that. Family members, when they talked of him, told how courtly his manners were and how deeply religious (Presbyterian) he was. Soon after the war he moved his family back to Alabama, settling at Bladon Springs, once known as the "Saratoga of the South." For a while he traveled about southwest Alabama, selling sewing machines. Or trying to sell them.

At one time he managed the warehouse at the steamboat landing on the Tombigbee River at Tuscahoma, in Choctaw County. My mother, Helen Gaines Tabb, was born at Tuscahoma on St. Valentine's Day, in 1882.

Grandmother Tabb taught school. Having no one to leave her youngest child, Helen, with, she took her to school. Mother recalled that the boys used to tease her by saying "She's a honey but the bees don't know it."

Grandmother Tabb also served meals to passengers waiting to board the steamboats at Tuscahoma (the boats made trips up-river from Mobile to Demopolis and back) and provided lodging for travelers.

Aunt Bet used to tell how, as a child, she would listen for whistles of the steamboats (she could identify each boat by the tone of its whistle) and would run to the landing to meet them. Often the captains brought her presents from Mobile, and occasionally she would be invited to ride up river with them.

It was while the Tabb family lived at Bladon Springs, in 1873, that three-year-old Emma Samuel and John Crenshaw, one month old, died of whooping cough. Their deaths came within a week of each other.

Later, when the family moved to the new town of Thomasville, in Clarke County, their twenty-four year old daughter Jessie Rebecca died of an undiagnosed fever, an illness that claimed the lives of a dozen young people in Thomasville that summer of 1889.

I know Aunt Jessie from her scrapbook of poems and of postcards; from squares of a quilt she made by gathering wild flowers and leaves and embroidering their outlines with careful stitches; and from her autograph album, dated 1882.

In Aunt Jessie's album were inscribed sentiments as innocent and flowery as the spray of red roses embossed on its cover.

Sweet beauty sleeps upon thy brow
And floats before my eyes.
As meek and pure as doves art thou
Or beings of the skies,

was penned in a flourishing hand by an admirer identified only as B.G.T.

E.M. Powe wrote, "May the roses of eternal happiness bloom ever in the garden of your destiny."

It was in March, 1883, that an anonymous friend in Tuscahoma wrote,

If every wish I have for thee
Was a bright and sparkling gem,
I'd place upon thy placid brow
A brilliant diadem.

The last entry in her album is dated August 10, 1889, less than three weeks before her death.

Grandmother Tabb was Postmaster when Jessie died. Grandfather "helped" her in the Post Office.

It may have been after the death of Jessie, or it may have been when her daughter, Annie Long Tucker, died in 1905, leaving three small children, that someone said to Grandmother, "O, Mrs. Tabb, you've had so much trouble."

"No," Grandmother replied, "I've had sorrows but not trouble —there is a great difference."

The only photograph I have of Grandmother Tabb shows her, a woman in her fifties, wearing a high necked black dress of silk moire, trimmed in jet beading. Her dark hair, parted in the middle, and pulled back from her big ears, is topped with a small black bonnet that matches her dress. Her mouth is firm, unsmiling. And her eyes are very sad.

Aunt Bet could be quite firm. There was no city delivery when she was postmaster, so the patrons came to the Post Office to get their mail. After the train arrived, and after Mr. Kirby Nichols (he wore a holstered pistol strapped around his waist to protect the mail, in accordance with postal regulations, but Aunt Bet forbade him to load the gun) had hauled the sacks of mail in his green, two-wheeled cart from the depot to the Post Office, folks would gather to wait for the mail to be distributed in the lock boxes.

First the letters were "put up," the term everybody used, then the newspapers, then notices of packages, and finally fourth class matter. There wasn't much of such trash mail back then. Aunt Bet always closed all the windows—the stamp window and the general delivery window and the money order window—while the mail was being put up.

The Post Office lobby was a social center of Thomasville. News was exchanged there, hunting and fishing stories told, dates made, parties planned and informal committee meetings held. Black-bordered funeral notices were posted there, too, with the full name of the deceased and the hour and location of the services.

Late one afternoon, while the mail from the last train of the day was being put up, the lobby was unusually crowded. Several groups of high school students were laughing and talking. The place was noisy.

Aunt Bet flung open the door to the lobby and commanded: "Be less quiet out there!".

There was instant silence. Her words may have been confused, but they were effective. And "Be less quiet" became a favorite expression in our family.

Aunt Bet's Post Office lobby was ominously quiet one morning when two political rivals chanced to meet there, face to face. One of them was my cousin, Earl Tucker, editor of our weekly newspaper.

Earl's race for a seat in the Alabama Legislature had been a bitter one, marked by ugly accusations and threats of violence on both sides. Friends of the candidates managed to keep them apart until that fateful morning at the Post Office.

Earl was taking his mail out of his box and replying to the banter of other folks in the lobby, when his opponent walked in. All conversation ceased. Two or three people sidled out of the door onto the sidewalk. The two men glared at each other.

Earl was the first to speak. "Take off your glasses!" he shouted. Seems he was under the impression that it was either illegal or unsportsmanlike to hit a man who was wearing glasses. It may have been. Anyhow, a scuffle followed and a lick or two was passed before bystanders separated the combatants.

Earl's opponent stormed out of the Post Office, vowing to go get his gun and kill Earl.

Earl walked down the street toward his newspaper office. If he planned to get his gun, he didn't say so. He had gone about a block when friends surrounded him and hustled him into the bank, where they locked him in the vault.

"Only safe place we could think of," they explained later. "He was about to get shot."

Earl spent several hours there in the dark, surrounded by safe deposit boxes and money, until mediators calmed his would-be assailant down. I can't remember whether he won that election or not, but I know he used to claim to be the only politician valuable enough to be locked in a bank vault.

There was an occasion back in the 1920s when Aunt Bet's firmness and determination almost led her to violence. The State Highway Department was building a new road, a graveled road, through Thomasville. Aunt Bet was pleased with this progress (Thomasville's streets were so muddy during wet weather that shoe shine boys used to chant, "Shine 'em up slick so the mud won't stick!"), but she was mightily upset when she learned that plans called for cutting down a row of old oak trees in front of the Methodist parsonage. Aunt Bet loved trees.

Despite her protests, the official word was, "The trees will be cut."

"They will *not* be cut," Aunt Bet declared.

So on the day when the highway crew was to arrive with saws and axes, Aunt Bet took a day off from the Post Office, moved a rocking chair to the shade of those oaks, put a shotgun across her lap and sat there all day long, rocking and crocheting. Nobody touched those trees. And, somehow, engineers later figured out a way to move the roadbed enough to save the oaks.

Aunt Bet staunchly denied another persistent family story that she, a very dressed-up and excited young lady about to see her first train, was warned, as that train puffed into sight, "You'd better let down your parasol; it might frighten the engine." And she did. She always said it never happened, but other family members declared it did.

She never denied the truth of the story about her train trip from Texas back to Alabama, however. She had been living in Texas with her husband, James Meigs Forster, and their little boy, Jamie, but she wanted to come back to Thomasville for the birth of her second baby.

All arrangements had been made for the trip: packing done, tickets bought, and the family back in Alabama notified of the arrival date. On the day before they were to leave Texas, four-year-old Jamie broke out with measles.

Aunt Bet never considered changing her plans. She just put a hat with a thick black veil on her young son, tied it securely in place and they rode the train those hundreds of miles from Texas to Alabama. Jamie never removed his veiled hat the entire trip.

Jamie, who grew up to be a dramatic and rather pompous man, never thought the story of his veiled train ride was the least bit funny, but the rest of the family did.

Aunt Bet was a joiner. She belonged to the Methodist Church (back then it was the Methodist Episcopal Church, South), the Daughters of the American Revolution, the United Daughters of the Confederacy, the Eastern Star, the Research Club (Thomasville's oldest federated Woman's Club), the Missionary Society, the Parent-Teacher Association (long after her own children were grown), and possibly other groups which I can't recall.

She had an assortment of pins, badges, buttons and ribbons stashed away in what she called her "puff box" on her marble-topped dresser, and, as the occasion required, she wore with pride the official ornamentation associated with each organization. Sometimes she let me play with them, pin them on and pretend I was a grown-up club lady.

Although Aunt Bet was proud of being a part of so many worthwhile groups, she was proudest of being the first woman in Clarke County to register to vote. And she not only registered, she voted in every election—always the straight Democratic ticket.

Aunt Bet was what was known as a "brag cook". Everything she cooked was good, but she was locally famous for her chicken salad, her hot tamales and her wedding cakes. She must have made at least a hundred wedding cakes.

There was no bakery in Thomasville, so when a bride-to-be began making her wedding plans, one of the first things she did was to hurry to the Post Office and call through the General Delivery window, "Miss Bettie, I'm going to get married! Will you please, ma'am, make my wedding cake for me? Mama said she'll have fresh eggs and butter for you to use." Aunt Bet believed in using plenty of both.

As a child, I'd lean against the edge of a metal-topped pine table in the kitchen and watch as Aunt Bet and Thurza made the cakes. Aunt Bet, a big bath towel pinned around her waist, measured and sifted (only Swan's Down Cake Flour would do for her cakes). Thurza's strong arm was called upon to do most of the creaming and beating, and it was Thurza who was entrusted with having the temperature in the wood stove exactly right. How she could judge the heat, I never understood. As they worked together, they often sang, the motions of the wire whisk and the kitchen spoon setting a rhythm for their duet. "Old Ship of Zion" was a favorite.

When the last of the batter was spooned into the three round, graduated cake pans, I was handed the bowl to lick. That treat was what I had been waiting for. As I ran my finger around the bowl to get the last taste of the rich batter, I was warned, "Remember to tiptoe in the kitchen. The cakes are in the oven, and we don't want them to fall. So tiptoe."

While I tiptoed (how many miles did I, the child, tiptoe across that rough kitchen floor?) I often wondered if God kept count of tiptoes. Thurza had told me once, "The hairs on your head is numbered, and God knows how many steps you take. When you takes all the steps God planned for you, that's when you gonna die." I walked backward a lot after that disclosure, hoping to confuse God.

Although Aunt Bet liked to bake cakes, it was decorating them that gave her real joy. She had no fancy paraphernalia. Someone gave her a decorating kit once, but she passed it on to me to make mud pies with. All she needed to create her masterpieces was a sheet of heavy white stationery rolled into a cone and filled with white icing. A snip or two with the kitchen scissors on the point of the cone created the opening through which she coaxed her designs.

Dainty lacework fences outlined the three tiers. Entwined hearts of tiny rosebuds peeped out from latticed backgrounds. Graceful vines with swirling leaves encircled each layer. I got to eat the icing left in the paper cones.

Aunt Bet would have been offended if anyone had offered to pay her for making cakes. To hear the bride exclaim, "O, it's perfect!" was all the compensation she wanted. There was one young bride who declared, "O, it's much too pretty to cut!" And, much to the dismay of the guests at the reception, she took the cake, whole, with her on her honeymoon.

I suppose the last wedding cake Aunt Bet made was for me, for my wedding, February 10, 1946. She was seventy-eight years old then and in poor health, and dear Thurza was no longer there to help her, but by doing a little at a time, resting between the decorating of each layer, she created a beautiful cake with all the rosebuds, leaves, trellises, and hearts that were her hallmark. If there were flaws, as she said there were, I could not see them for my tears of love and joy.

So many stories about Aunt Bet!

Her mastery of cooking was widely known, but not many people knew of her skill at making wine. This was more than fifty years ago, back when the Methodist Episcopal Church, South— where Aunt Bet sang alto in the choir every Sunday morning— was staunchly opposed to the use of spirits, even wine. So Aunt Bet didn't talk much about her wine-making.

Well, one late spring Sunday, when the blackberries were just at the right stage, Aunt Bet came home from church with her mind set on spending the afternoon making wine.

She had the berries in a cheese cloth bag and was in the process of squeezing them, her hands already stained deep purple by the juice, when she heard someone knocking on the front door. She fanned the fruit flies away, peeped down the hall and saw her preacher and the chairman of the Board of Stewards at the door. Obviously she was in something of a predicament, but, as always, Aunt Bet was resourceful, prepared for any eventuality. She, fortunately, had left her hat and white gloves on a chair in the back hall when she came home from church.

"Coming!", she called.

She shut the kitchen door firmly, hoping the fruit flies would stay put, picked up her gloves and put them on her stained hands as she hurried to greet her guests. If the preacher and the chairman of the board thought it strange that Aunt Bet had on an apron (she had somehow forgotten to take it off) and white gloves on a Sunday afternoon, they didn't comment on it. What they had come for, they said, was to ask Aunt Bet to serve on the Board of Stewards. She thanked them for the compliment and said she'd let them know.

"I decided," she confessed later, "that if my wine turned out well, I'd serve on the board."

It must have been a good year for blackberry wine! Aunt Bet was a member of the Board of Stewards until her death at age ninety-four.

There was one period when Aunt Bet actually owned a church. About 1930, when I was twelve, she and Tabb built a house on the street back of our house, and moved out of the room on the ell where they had lived since before I was born. Aunt Bet drew the plans for her house on the back of a brown grocery bag, and Mr. Jim Bishop built it for $2,500.00. The house was a brick veneer bungalow with seven rooms, a wide hall and a concrete porch on the north side. Aunt Bet always used the adjective in speaking of that porch. "Let's go sit on the North porch," she would say on a sultry summer night, and somehow the very words made us feel ten degrees cooler.

There was a big vacant lot across the street from Aunt Bet's house, and soon after she and Tabb moved, the Holy Rollers put up a tent and began holding nightly services on that lot. The congregation's religious fervor was expressed in outbursts of shouting that continued far into the night. The racket was so great that Aunt Bet and Tabb were often kept awake until after midnight.

Aunt Bet did not wish to offend the worshippers, most of whom she knew well, by having their services declared a public nuisance, so she just bought the property.

She took a lot of teasing about that purchase. "What time are you preaching tonight, Miss Bettie?" she was asked. Aunt Bet just smiled and enjoyed her peaceful sleep.

Later she rented the lot to a man who built Thomasville's first and only miniature golf course there. Part of the rental agreement was that play would cease by 9:30 P.M. and that I would be permitted to play free. I thought Aunt Bet made a wonderful swap.

It was about this time that Aunt Bet introduced me to O-Do-Ro-No. We were sitting in Tabb's Buick in front of People's Drug Store, waiting for Clayton Megginson to bring out the Coca-Colas we had ordered. Aunt Bet, who had a keen sense of smell, sniffed in my direction, and, after a moment, said "Katink," (her pet name for me) "I think you and I need to go make a purchase in the drug store."

So we went in (Tabb promised not to drink our Coca-Colas— we called them "dopes" back then) and Aunt Bet bought me a bottle of O-Do-Ro-No, my first deodorant. It was a thick pink liquid in a clear glass bottle, and it was applied to the underarm area with a small round sponge attached to the screw cap by a metal wire, an apparatus similar to a shoe polish applicator.

The O-Do-Ro-No was effective, but it took a long time to dry. I remember walking around my room (I kept the bottle on the green washstand, beside the silver birthday mug that held my Prophylactic tooth brush and Forham's tooth paste) with my arms outstretched like a bird poised for flight. If the deodorant was not perfectly dry, it would eat holes in your clothes. I don't know why it didn't gnaw into my flesh.

Aunt Bet loved pretty things, and, as she grew older and more financially secure, she bought jewelry, furniture, especially antique pieces, china and silver. Perhaps growing up in the hard times of Reconstruction, when her family had so little in the way of worldly possessions, prompted her to want nice things.

One of her early purchases was a rectangular rosewood piano, trimmed with brass beading and with wide bands of engraved brass circling its carved legs. Its long drawers held a clutter of old sheet music, used candles, bridge cards (many decks) with score pads, pencils, and picture post cards from vacationing family and friends. It was never tuned, but its volume of sound was so low that my playmates and I could bang on it whenever we wanted to without danger of disturbing the grown-ups.

One of the most avid piano players was C. M. Dendy, about my age, who lived around the corner and up the hill from our house. C. M.'s favorite piece was a song called "Maggie" which he sang as he "played." I've forgotten the words, but it was a dialogue between a mother and her daughter which began:

Maggie!
Yes, ma'am.
Come right up stairs.
Maggie!
Yes, ma'am.
Come say your prayers.

C. M. knew all the words, and he sang and played "Maggie" so often that the old piano became known as the Maggie Box.

It's in my daughter's house now, still untuned and still called the Maggie Box, though it has been more than sixty years since anyone played "Maggie" on it.

When she was eighty four years old, Aunt Bet broke her hip, and she spent the rest of her life—ten years—in bed.

Logically, the stories about Aunt Bet should have ended, or at least dwindled off then, but they didn't. Aunt Bet never thought of herself as an invalid, so nobody else did either. She just wasn't as active physically as she once was. After she was bed-ridden and could no longer visit antique dealers, jewelry stores and gift shops, Aunt Bet became more and more interested in mail order catalogues.

She began sending off for vases, bowls, china demi-tasse cups, silver souvenir spoons, beads, commemorative plates, figurines, candlesticks, folding fans, bracelets, decorated boxes, gold pins— whatever caught her fancy. She called her purchases her "pretties."

At first she showed off her pretties with pride, but when some family members began to hint that she was wasting money, was being extravagant, she became more secretive about her purchases. After she and Heatha, her nurse and co-conspirator, had unwrapped and admired the contents of each package, they'd wrap it back up and hide it under Aunt Bet's big bed.

For years after Aunt Bet died, we found gifts for showers, weddings, birthdays and graduations from the store of pretties she left under her bed.

In addition to her mail-ordering, Aunt Bet did exquisite handwork, propped up on her pillows there in bed in the front room. She liked that room, that room where she could look out the windows and watch the cars pass on the highway and see visitors coming up the front walk. She had lots of visitors. One day when she was in her nineties, I walked into her room and found her intent on making a list.

"What are you doing?" I asked.

"I'm making a list of all the men who've been to see me in the last year. I'm not counting the ones who came with their wives, or the preachers—just the men who came because they wanted to come." She had nearly one hundred names on that list, a serigamy of visitors.

She did have an assortment of friends. There was Mr. Frank Beck, a sort of a hermit who lived at Beck's Landing on the Alabama River and would come by to see her when he walked into town on business. Mr. Beck always needed a shave. His shirt and khaki pants were dirty, and his hat looked as if it had fallen into and been fished out of the muddy river at least a hundred times.

He carried a croaker sack over his shoulder, a sack full of clatters and lumps, that he put down outside the front door. I'd seen Mr. Beck ever since I was a child, and I'd always heard he carried trot lines and pistols and canned salmon in his sack. I was scared to ask. Or to peep.

I was amazed when Aunt Bet told me Mr. Beck had been to college, that he could read a little Greek and Latin. Aunt Bet was proud of having read Caesar, Virgil, and Cicero by the time she was twelve. However, judging by the tempo of their conversation and their laughter, I don't believe Aunt Bet and Mr. Beck discussed Latin classics when he came visiting.

And there was Willie Grady Brasell, who used to come in from the country with bundles of fat pine kindling to start the fires in her grate. Willie Grady had been a rural mail carrier for a long time, so they had a lot to talk about. He reported on news of families along his route, all Aunt Bet's friends.

Several young men came by rather often—not as a group—bearing gifts of wine and beer, carefully concealed in heavy paper bags. "My thoughtful young bootleggers," Aunt Bet called them. Indeed they were. Thomasville was in a dry county (sales of alcoholic beverages were illegal there), so these young men brought spirits back to Aunt Bet when business took them to Selma or Montgomery, or other cities where beer and wine were available. Aunt Bet's doctor had prescribed an occasional glass of wine or bottle of beer, and Aunt Bet was happy to follow his prescription.

Aunt Bet was drinking one of those bottles of beer one Sunday morning while she listened to the church service on her bedside radio, as was her custom. She was singing along with the choir, using her leather bound hymnal with her name embossed in gold, and Tabb was back in the kitchen, fixing her dinner (midday) tray.

"Tabb! Come here quick," Aunt Bet called. "I've spilled beer all over my hymnal!"

Aunt Bet, a naturally hospitable person, did not welcome visits from certain pious fundamentalist church members. "They talk about saving souls just like they'd been out picking up hickory nuts," she used to say. "And I don't like being counted as anybody's good deed for the day!"

One day three of the good ladies came calling. After an exchange of pleasantries, one of them asked, "Miss Bettie, have you made your peace with the Lord?"

"We've never had a falling out," Aunt Bet replied. And she got busy with her knitting.

Piano Lessons

MOST MEMBERS of my family were musical (Daddy could play the mouth organ and dance at the same time), so Mother assumed that I had musical talent, too. She was mistaken.

The first intimation I had that I was about to be launched on a musical career came when I arrived home from school one afternoon and found Blind Gates (I called him Mr. Blind Gates) tuning the upright piano in our living room.

"Why are you having the piano tuned?" I asked Mother.

"You're going to take music lessons," she replied. "It will be so nice when you learn to play pretty pieces on the piano, won't it?"

"I guess so," I said. From the very first, I was not enthusiastic about those lessons.

Mother had chosen as my teacher (actually there wasn't much choice in Thomasville, though I still believe she made the poorest possible one) one of Daddy's distant relatives, Cousin Golda.

Cousin Golda was a well-trained musician, held office in the Missionary Society on the local, district, and conference level, and was undeniably a good woman. I hated her.

The afternoon I reported for my first lesson, the room was so dark it took me several seconds to find my teacher. Then I heard her rasping voice coming from the shadows near the corner of the piano.

"Sit right here, Kathryn," she said.

I sat. The piano stool was hard and wobbly and squeaked whenever I moved.

"You will sit still so the stool will not squeak," Cousin Golda said. "Do you understand?"

"Yes, ma'am."

Heavy draperies at the two windows prevented the entrance of any natural light, and the room's only illumination came from a tall floor lamp with a handpainted glass shade hung with silk tassels.

In my childish ignorance, I had assumed that I would be taught immediately to play tuneful pieces. Cousin Golda dispelled such notions. She gave me to understand that "pieces" were in the distant future. Scales and exercises came first. My coordination was poor, the only notes I was ever sure of were those in the octave above middle C (locating middle C was not always easy), and my sense of timing was terrible. No matter how vigorously Cousin Golda intoned, "One-two-three-four! One-two-three-four!" I always lagged between two and three and was hopelessly behind by the count of four. I suppose it is no wonder that Cousin Golda occasionally rapped my fumbling fingers with the long pencil she used for beating time.

I could forgive her the finger-rapping, but I could never forgive her for cutting off the lower limbs of the big oak tree in her front yard. Climbing that tree was the one thing I had to look forward to on my twice-weekly sessions with Cousin Golda. By standing on her picket fence, I could reach the lower limbs of the tree, swing myself up and climb to the tip-top where I could see all over town: the two churches, the railroad depot, the lumber yard, the stores—everything. The world was peaceful and bright and beautiful up there among the leaves.

Then one afternoon Cousin Golda walked out on her front porch to call me in for my lesson (I had been late the lesson before because I had to fill in for a missing player at a sandlot football game I happened to pass), and she found me up in her tree.

The lower limbs were hacked off before my next lesson. Cousin Golda said it was a safety measure. I knew it wasn't.

My music lessons filled me with such dread I would do almost anything to escape them. I remember once the county Health Officer came to our school and gave the assembled grammar school pupils a talk on personal hygiene and the importance of a healthy body.

At the end of his talk, he asked if any children wanted to be vaccinated for smallpox. I was at the head of the line—it was music lesson day. I figured by the time school was out I'd have such a bad reaction from the vaccination that I wouldn't have to face the piano keyboard or Cousin Golda.

The only reaction I had was from Mother, who was horrified that I had been vaccinated at school, free. "Our family doctor handles all health-related matters for us," she reminded me. "Vaccinated at school! The very idea!"

Off to music I went. I still bear the scar of that vaccination. And my piano lessons.

The piano lessons, however, were delightfully pleasant episodes compared with the semi-annual horrors known as recitals. At least Cousin Golda and I were the only ones who suffered through my lessons. Family and friends shared my shame at recitals. On those occasions, Cousin Golda opened the double doors between the living room and dining room, pushed the furniture against the wall and arranged rows of chairs for her guests.

I'll never understand why I was permitted, much less required, to appear on those programs. On the morning of the event, I'd begin praying for something to save me: serious illness, a broken arm, a terrible tornado. Anything. But my prayers went unanswered.

At the appointed time, I would walk out, announce the name of my piece (not even the composer would have recognized it otherwise), seat myself on the squeaky stool and begin to play. The first four or five measures of "Airy Fairies" usually went fairly well, but after that hopeful beginning, I always forgot my piece, blundered to a discordant ending and hurried, teary-eyed, from the room.

During the refreshment hour (Cousin Golda always served weak punch and pimento cheese sandwiches cut in triangles), other mothers heard:

"Evelyn played beautifully today, you must be very proud of her."

Or: "I always look forward to Ruth's part on the program. She is so talented!"

My mother had to content herself with hearing, "Such a pretty dress Kathryn has on. So becoming. Did you make it?"

My deliverance came from an unexpected source, one I had never thought to pray for. We were getting ready for bed one night when the mill whistle gave three long blasts, the signal for the volunteer fire department to report for duty. I ran out in the back yard to try to locate the blaze. "It's Cousin Golda's house! Cousin Golda's!" I called back as I ran toward the burning house.

When I got there, the roof was burning all over, and I heard the fire chief (he ran the shoe shop when he wasn't fighting fires) say, "Looks like a goner. We'd better see what furniture we can save."

The flames lighted up the front rooms of the house. I watched the men gather up tables, chairs, beds, trunks, books and clothes, and hand them to neighbors who took them across the street, over to the Gunns' back yard, out of the range of falling sparks. While the furniture was being carried out, Cousin Golda's husband, Hadley, was running around the outside of the house asking the firemen, "Have you saved my Revolutionary relics? Have you saved my Revolutionary relics?" I'm not sure any of them knew what he was talking out.

In all the excitement, I had not even thought of Cousin Golda until I heard the fire chief say to her, "I'm sorry, Miss Golda, but I'm afraid that's all we can do. We got nearly everything out except the piano."

The piano!

I moved around to where I could see the living room. The room was alive with light, brighter than it had ever been before, and the flames were already devouring the ugly piano.

It was the most beautiful sight I'd ever seen.

Methodists and Baptists

THE METHODIST CHURCH, a white frame building with high concrete steps and a tall steeple, was one block from our house. My family was present every time the bell in that steeple summoned worshippers. If we got there early enough, I was lifted up by Daddy so I could pull the bell rope.

Though I was taken to church from infancy, I was not christened there. I received this rite, so I am told, on our front porch with only our family and the officiating minister present. Having my christening at home may have been a compromise between my father, brought up in the Baptist tradition opposed to "infant baptism", and my Presbyterian-reared mother. Perhaps Mother feared that I would not behave well in public. I don't know— and there's no one left to ask.

Although I did not embarrass my family at my christening, I was something of an embarrassment to them at church some two or three years later. It was about 1921, the beginning of the Jazz Age, the era of the Flapper, the Roaring Twenties. The Shimmy was a new and shocking dance. Unbeknownst to my parents, Thurza taught me to shimmy. There in the privacy of the kitchen, she showed me how to shake my hips in time to the fast rhythm she patted. She even took me down to her house (within calling distance of our side porch) where her husband, Alex, fiddled a tune for me to shimmy by.

Well, one Sunday morning we had special music in our church. "Miss Annie" Kirk, who played the piano (it was an old upright, and every summer Sunday a stiff bunch of zinnias from Mrs. Mackey's garden sat on it) at all our services, was joined by her visiting sister-in-law, Estelle, a violinist of some renown from Birmingham.

I had never heard any musical instrument except a piano in church, so as soon as Estelle began to play, I hopped up on the bench between Mother and Daddy and announced in a loud voice, "I'll shimmy for you!"

Mother grabbed me up and hustled me out of the church before my performance got underway.

To be truthful, I do not recall this episode, but I have heard about it often enough to make me sure it did happen. I might have been a famous dancer if my premier performance had not been squelched. I never danced—or tried to dance—in public again.

Usually Mother kept me quiet in church by letting me play with two tiny china dolls, a little girl and a little boy. They were two inches tall, their arms moved, and their cloth clothes were glued on. The dolls lived all week wrapped in a handkerchief in Mother's purse, and were only brought out at the beginning of the sermon each Sunday. I still have the little girl doll (she has a green china bow in her hair), but her companion has disappeared.

After I had outgrown the doll stage, I entertained myself by watching the people. Mother and Daddy disapproved of letting children draw or color in church. We didn't have any church bulletins to draw on anyhow.

Dr. Richard Irons, our family doctor, was one of my favorites to watch. He sat in a small bench beside a window in the back of the church, in case he was called out during the service.

Our church had no air-conditioning (nobody had it back then), and we didn't even have ceiling fans. On summer Sundays that sanctuary was hot. Dr. Irons sweated more than anybody I ever saw. On those hot Sundays, he would wipe his face, neck and arms with a big handkerchief, and then he would lean out the window, pushing aside the leaves of the sumac tree (I thought it was "shoemake" until I was grown), and wring the sweat out. Then he'd drape the handkerchief over the back of the bench to dry until he needed it again. Some Sundays, especially in late August, he'd wring that handkerchief out six or eight times during the sermon.

Dr. Irons could also drive a car backwards faster than anybody I ever knew. Our doctors made house calls then, and Dr. Irons often backed five or six blocks, at full speed, from one patient's home to another. He said it was quicker than turning around. Other drivers learned to get out of his way. He usually walked to church, so I didn't get to observe his backing skills there.

I did observe, every Sunday, a maiden lady whose name I have now forgotten, who sat down the bench from us. She had a front tooth missing, and to hide this defect she fashioned a tooth of beeswax. During the sermon, she would chew the wax tooth. While the benediction was being pronounced, she would shape the moist wax into a tooth again and stick it back in place. I peeped. Every Sunday.

The Philen sisters, Miss Sarah and Miss Rebecca, occupied the same bench over on the right hand side of the church for sixty years or more. They were faithful in attendance though when I knew them they were both so deaf they never heard a word of the sermon. They were inclined to nod (I knew who habitually slept in church and could almost predict in what order they would drop off), but they were vigilant in keeping each other awake. "Sister! Sister! You're starting to snore," one would say to the other in a loud voice.

Daddy would give me a stern look to keep me from giggling, but his eyes were laughing—and I knew we would talk about the Philen sisters at our dinner table.

I was sure somebody would tell again about the Sunday Miss Sarah asked, "Sister, how much longer you think he's going to preach? My stomach is just a-growling."

But my favorite church story is about the Sunday the stovepipe fell. Our church was heated by a big pot-bellied stove that stood near the rear of the sanctuary. On cold Sundays, Moody Drinkard or Tom Hadley Tyson would go early and build a fire in that stove (they also built fires in smaller stoves and lit kerosene heaters in the Sunday School classrooms) so that the sanctuary would be warm when the first worshippers arrived. The stovepipe did not go out the roof above the stove. It ran, suspended by wires, along the high ceiling, almost the entire length of the sanctuary, until it exited to the right of the pulpit.

Well, one hot July Sunday, when Dr. Irons had already wrung his handkerchief out twice, a joint of that stovepipe came loose, and a peck of soot—the accumulation of years—cascaded down through that dangling pipe onto my playmate, Teace Cleiland.

Teace was the blondest little girl I ever knew. She was what we called tow-headed, a pure and natural platinum, and her skin was so fair it looked as if she really had spent her life in the shade of a magnolia tree. That Sunday she was wearing a new white voile dress, one her grandmother had made for her, with pale blue smocking that matched her eyes.

One minute she was sitting there in church as pretty and pious as you please. The next minute she and her dress were black with soot, solid black. She wasn't hurt at all, just startled and frightened.

The preacher pronounced a quick benediction, and announced something about services that night, but nobody heard what he said. Nearly everybody was clustered around Teace, trying to soothe her and get her out of the church.

Little wisps of soot continued to drift out of the broken pipe. Mighty few people escaped getting smutty. Not as smutty as Teace, but smutty. Mr. Vince McDonald, who owned the Thomasville Pressing Club (why did they call dry cleaning establishments "pressing clubs"?) had the biggest business week he had ever had. As I recall, we Methodists worshipped with the Baptists that Sunday night after the stovepipe fell.

Teace and I were in the same Sunday School class, though she was some two years younger than I was. Her sister, Evelyn, and I were the same age, but Teace always played with us and went everywhere we went. We never complained. In fact, I often liked Teace better than I did Evelyn.

When Evelyn and I were toddlers, she leaned out of her buggy right in front of the Methodist Church, and bit a plug out of my cheek. I don't remember the incident, of course, but I carried the scar until I was grown. She and I had just been to Sunday School (nursery department) and it could have been, as her mother said, that she was trying to kiss me. I doubt it, though.

Evelyn, Teace, other Methodist children and I attended Sunday School there in that white frame church until we went off to college. I have a stack of promotion certificates (most of them have a colored picture of Jesus with little children on them) indicating that I moved forward in my Sunday classes, but I can't recall being inspired by any of my teachers.

In fact, the only Biblical knowledge that I remember from Sunday School came in Miss Julia Mary Allen's class when I was in the first grade. We met in the rear of the sanctuary where two improvised classrooms were curtained off with heavy brown burlap.

What Miss Allen taught me was the Bible Alphabet:

A. A soft answer turneth away wrath.

B. Be not hasty in thy spirit to be angry.

C. Christ Jesus came into the world to save sinners.

D. Do unto others as ye would have them do unto you.

After almost sixty-five years, I remember them all, even: "X— Exercise loving kindness."

Maybe I learned something about moral living at Sunday School. I'm not sure. I already knew the Bible stories (Daddy brought me a new Bible story book every time he came home from a trip), and I seem to have learned young how Methodists are supposed to conduct themselves in Sunday School.

They say that before the time I was learning the Bible Alphabet, we had a visitor in our Sunday School class, a very obstreperous little boy. After our patient teacher had made several attempts to correct his behaviour, attempts which served only to make him more boisterous, I offered a simple solution:

"Send him to the Baptists," I said.

It's another of the episodes in my early life I don't actually remember but have heard told countless times.

Our Methodist Church in Thomasville didn't celebrate homecomings or have dinners-on-the-ground, but my family was not deprived of the pleasure of such occasions. Country churches all around Thomasville invited us to their observances. My favorite was Bethel, a one-room frame Methodist Church just over the line in Marengo County. We always took a big basket of food, of course, fried chicken and stuffed eggs, and one of Aunt Bet's three-layer caramel cakes and such, to add to the noontime feast spread on the long, shady tables. Daddy always insisted on taking a big block of ice wrapped in several thicknesses of newspapers and croaker sacks. Ice was hard to come by out there in the country, and Daddy's ice brought welcome coolness to many a tub of lemonade and tea (well sweetened).

I remember families at Bethel who brought dinner in trunks. On the bottom were fried chicken, chicken pie, barbecue, fresh vegetables, cornbread, tomatoes. The tray of the trunk held pies, some with meringue two inches high. I always scouted around to see who brought chess pie, my favorite.

For many years, the homecoming sermon was preached by the Rev. William Hasty, an elderly man when I first knew him. He seemed to have shrunk away from his clothes, leaving great gaps around his shirt collar and around the top of his trousers. His grey suspenders held him and his clothing together.

Preacher Hasty's false teeth did not fit well. Like his clothes, they were too big. When he preached, which he did with devout fervor, his ill-fitting dentures gave all his S's a loud hissing sound. He seemed unaware of this speech defect as he hissed through his favorite sermon topic, "The Serpent of Sin."

One homecoming Sunday at Bethel, it rained. Hard. At noon time, the worshippers brought their food into the church and spread it on the handmade benches. Preacher Hasty ate heartily. (I was always amazed at the small man's appetite). When he had finished, he walked over to an open window, removed his teeth and held them out so the rain could wash them off.

Preacher Hasty lived to be a very old man. During his final illness, one of his daughters wrote a postcard to report on his condition. "Papa is low sick," the card said. "He can neither speak nor spit."

That phrase, "speak nor spit," became for our family a gauge for the seriousness of all illnesses.

In addition to the religious instruction I received at home, Sunday School and church services, I sometimes attended sessions of camp meetings at Dixon's Mills, some twelve miles from Thomasville. The camp ground was on the bank of a creek. Frame cottages, some of them whitewashed, lined a wide street leading to the open tabernacle where services were held three times daily.

It was in that tabernacle that I, about eight years old, heard the evangelist say, "Now, I want you who are saved to stand up and tell when you were born again." All around the tabernacle I watched men and women stand up and heard them—so many of them—say, "I was born again under the preaching of Reverend Lee Tucker."

A woman sitting down the row from me leaned over and whispered to me, "That's your grandfather they're talking about, Reverend Tucker. He was a fine preacher."

I have four things that belonged to my grandfather, James Lee Tucker: an oak rocking chair he made himself; a hunting horn with his initials, 1883, and a crude outline of a church scratched on it; a double-barrelled, rabbit-eared shotgun; and his Bible.

The Bible may have been the one he wrapped up in his clothes and tied to his horse's saddle the blustery day he and his horse swam the Tombigbee River. Grandfather was a circuit-riding Baptist preacher, and he lived at Nanafalia, in Marengo County. One Sunday, the story goes, he had a preaching appointment at a little Baptist Church over in Choctaw County, across the river.

When he, riding the horse that had taken him to so many preaching appointments, reached the river, he found that high waters had washed the ferry away.

"I'm sorry," the ferryman told him, "but you can't get across today. The river's out of its banks and mighty swift. Guess you'll have to find a church on this side of the 'Bigbee to preach in!"

"My congregation is expecting me in Choctaw County," Grandfather replied.

So he rode his horse along the river bank to an isolated spot, out of sight of anybody, took off all his clothes, wrapped his Bible up in them and tied the bundle to his horse's saddle. Then he led the horse into the water, and the two of them swam across the muddy, turbulent stream.

When they reached the other side, Grandfather dried off on bear grass, put on his clothes, placed his Bible under his arm and rode off to fill his appointment. There likely weren't more than twenty-five folks in his congregation that day. But those worshippers were expecting him. I hope the Bible he preached from that Sunday is the one I have.

The rocking chair is the one I remember seeing Grandfather sitting in. He was a tall, gaunt man, his legs hardly bigger around than the legs of the chair, and he had a long white beard. He seemed to sort of fold up like a grasshopper when he sat in that chair.

There's a story in our family about how Grandfather used to sit out on his front porch (the porch faced west) late in the afternoons with his watch in one hand and his almanac in the other, checking to make sure God let the sun go down on time.

After I was grown, a man who had known my grandfather well, had lived near him in Nanafalia, told me a strange story.

"One sultry spring day," he said, "I was working in the field with my papa. I was a boy, about half grown.

"Suddenly the sky got black and everything got still. Real still. Papa hollered, 'Looks like a tornado coming—run for the house!'

"We couldn't get to the house before the storm hit, had to stop at the barn. We peeped through the cracks and saw this funnel cloud coming right at us. The wind was fierce and the barn was beginning to shake.

"I looked out again and I saw your grandfather, Reverend

Tucker, standing out in his cow lot. The wind was whipping his hair and his beard, and he was holding on tight to the top rail of the fence.

"His eyes were closed and his face was turned toward Heaven. I wanted to yell at him to open his eyes and see the tornado heading toward him, wanted to warm him, but he couldn't hear above the mighty wind.

"Then, with Papa, my brothers and me looking straight at it, that tornado turned and headed in the opposite direction! Nobody was even hurt. The only damage was to a stand of scrub timber.

"Your Grandfather purely prayed that tornado away. Prayed it away."

I wish I could have asked my grandfather about that experience. I don't remember that Grandfather ever said anything to me, can't recall the sound of his voice. Surely he spoke to me on those Sunday afternoons when we rode down to Grove Hill to visit him and Grandmother, but I was eager to go play with the cousins—Elizabeth, Willie Lee, Roy, Jack, Ethel and Tommy— out in the backyard, and probably did not listen.

Grandmother, a portly woman with her white hair piled atop her head, never failed to warn us cousins about climbing in the huge mulberry tree in the backyard, and, when the purple berries were ripe, to remind us that "eating those mulberries will give you worms." We always climbed the tree, and we also ate the berries. Not one of us ever had worms, not that I know of. Before the afternoon was over, the bottoms of our bare feet were deep purple from stepping on the ripe, fallen berries, and, no matter how careful we were, our clothes bore the indelible stains of the purple fruit.

We washed our feet and dabbed at the stains on our clothes with water from the bored well on the back porch. Unlike our dug well, my grandparents' bored well (I thought for a long time it was a "board" well, though I saw no reason for the name: no planks were in evidence) had a long, skinny bucket with a trap door in the bottom that closed when the bucket was full and the rope was pulled upward.

"You don't have to worry about children falling into a bored well," Grandmother used to say. I suppose she had enough to worry about with the hazards of the mulberry tree, falls and worms and such. She never seemed as concerned about the purple splotches on our clothes as our mothers did.

It was the water from that well on his back porch that Grandfather Tucker kept calling for during his final illness. But no matter how much water he drank, he kept begging for more. Daddy said Grandfather was delirious, and was reliving his months of captivity in a Yankee prison on Ship Island in 1864. There was never enough drinking water—or food—for the prisoners, and memories of those endless, sultry, thirsty days on that Mississippi coastal island haunted Grandfather until he drew his final breath in the little town of Grove Hill, Alabama, some sixty years later.

I remember going to Grandfather Tucker's funeral at Shiloh Baptist Church, a one-room country church in Marengo County where he had once been pastor. It was hot, August hot, inside the church. My father, carrying out Grandfather's request, read the Twenty-third Psalm. Several preachers eulogized "our departed brother," and as their talks stretched on, I, a child of six or seven, began to get restless. Mother whispered that I could go outside and play, so I tiptoed down the aisle (I had on my black patent leather shoes that Thurza had polished with half a biscuit), past row after row of mourners, sitting on splintery, angular pine benches, and out the door.

"Play quietly," Mother had said, so I sat on the wooden steps a few minutes trying to decide what to do. The church was built on rock pillars, high enough off the ground for a child to play under. I crawled beneath the edge of the church and knelt on the dry, grey sand there. From where I knelt, I could look across to the graveyard, see its rows of mounded graves, the granite markers, the Cape Jasmine and arborvitae bushes framed by the pillars of the church.

I began building a miniature graveyard of my own, mounding

graves in the sand, marking each one with a cross of oak twigs. A dozen or so tiny graves had been completed, and I was decorating them with leaves and yellow flowers from bitterweeds when I heard the shuffling of feet above my head and muffled voices singing "Abide With Me." I hummed along, as I crept out from under the church, being careful not to crack my head on the hand-hewn sills. I brushed the dirt off my hands and knees and watched as the pallbearers carried Grandfather's coffin out of the church.

Daddy took my hand when he came down the steps, and I walked between him and Mother, behind the pallbearers, to the open grave. I wondered if anyone would find my graveyard under the church.

My Parents

MY FATHER, JAMES WILSON TUCKER, was the oldest of my Grandfather Tucker's ten sons. Daddy was born in 1866, the year after Grandfather walked back home to Marengo County from the Yankee prison on Ship Island, off the Mississippi Coast, at the end of the War of Yankee Aggression. Grandfather walked back to the same dirt farm, the same life of hardship, he had left (what dreams of glory, what bursts of patriotism enticed him to enlist?) when he marched away at age eighteen to join the Confederate Army. He and Catherine Stafford were married in 1865. She, Catherine, died after the birth of their second son, Adlai. Grandfather married again in 1873, taking as his wife Miss Elizabeth Woodall Busbee, an Episcopalian school teacher from Mobile, who bore him eight sons.

"We always had more children than money," Grandfather used to say. Farming and preaching and sawmilling weren't lucrative occupations during Reconstruction. Daddy helped with the farming. He went to school only three months in his entire life, but he learned to read, and he believed that reading opened the doors to endless knowledge. So he read, always.

There wasn't a public library in Thomasville, not even one at school, but we had hundreds of books in the glass-front cases along our living room walls: a brown-bound set of Dickens, Stoddard's Lectures with their accounts of far away places, Irving S. Cobb, the English poets next to James Whitcomb Riley, the fifty-plus volumes of the Harvard Classics, Mark Twain, Zane Grey, Harold Bell Wright, John Trotwood Moore, Edgar Rice Burroughs, Henry W. Longfellow, Thomas Dixon, Augusta Evans Wilson, John Fox, Jr., Memorial Records of Alabama, Sir Walter Scott, a set of Our Wonder World, Edgar Allen Poe—all crowded together in those bookcases. Daddy read them all.

I knew what many of those writers looked like. Their pictures were on the cards we played "Authors" with. Playing Authors wasn't as much fun as playing Rook, and, as I recall, Daddy never played Authors, but he could beat everybody playing checkers or Rook or dominoes. He liked to win.

Maybe Daddy got enough of farming when he was a boy. We always had a garden, but Daddy never worked in it. It was Prince who took care of our garden, Prince and his mule. On a morning when the promise of spring stirred the trees' bare branches, the kind of morning that prompted Mother to buy cloth to cover the porch cushions, Prince would appear in the back yard and instruct Thurza, "Tell Mr. Jim I come to plow our garden."

The garden was behind the peach orchard, beyond the two pecan trees ("Spring has really come when pecan trees bud," Daddy used to say. "Pecan trees wait until the danger of freezing is past before they put out any leaves"), beyond the Q, beyond the chicken yard.

Prince let me help him plow, let me hold the wooden handles, worn slick and smooth by his rough hands.

"Careful, now," Prince would warn as I stumbled along the uneven furrows, or tripped over clods of freshly turned dirt. "Careful. Watch where you puts your feets."

As I watched, I found treasures for my playhouse: pieces of broken china, bits of colored glass, even an occasional marble. Prince put them in his pocket for me.

Prince found earthworms. He would reach down quickly, pick up the worms, writhing in anger over being disturbed by the plow, and put them in a Prince Albert tobacco can.

"Going fishing when I get through plowing our garden. Catch some big fish with these fat worms. Maybe I take you with me sometime." But he never did.

He did let me guide the mule with the frayed plow line, and he taught me to give the proper commands: "Whoa! Gee! Haw! Giddap."

"You got to speak out like you means it," Prince told me. "Mule ain't gonna pay no 'tention 'less you speak out. Folks ain't either," he added.

Daddy usually came out to check on the progress of the plowing before he went to the bank, but he left the gardening entirely up to Prince.

The only thing I ever knew Daddy to plant was kudzu. And he spent the rest of his life regretting it.

We had a coal pile and a wood pile out in the back yard. Daddy believed in having plenty of wood (my older brothers used to say that Daddy made them move the woodpile, stacking it neatly, from one side of the yard to the other every Saturday to keep them out of mischief) and coal on hand. Wood was readily available, but the local dealer occasionally ran out of coal: the Southern Railway's coal cars from Birmingham did not always arrive on schedule. So Daddy liked to keep a good supply in our yard.

Mother used to complain, especially during the summertime, about how unsightly the coal pile was. "It just looks so ugly out there in the back yard," she'd say.

So one day Daddy came home to dinner with about a half dozen small plants in his hand.

"Brought you a present," he told Mother. "Something to hide the coal pile. It's a miracle vine. They say it will grow ten feet a day, but I don't believe such a tale. Anyhow, the County Agent gave me these samples, and I thought I'd plant them around the coal pile. Maybe the vines will cover it before the summer is over. They call it kudzu."

So Daddy planted the kudzu. And in a few weeks it did cover the coal pile. It also covered the woodpile, the back fence and the side of the garage. It raced in all directions, reaching out to smother the peach orchard, the Q, my playhouse, even the chicken coops.

Late every afternoon, Daddy would go out to fight the kudzu. "I cut it back, and it catches me before I can get to the house," he used to say. Mother didn't have to complain about the coal pile being unsightly. It disappeared completely under a snarl of kudzu.

Somebody suggested that Daddy get a goat to graze the kudzu, keep it in check, but Mother vetoed that suggestion. There had been a goat on the premises before.

I must have been about five or six years old when Daddy called on the telephone to tell Mother he had a billy goat for me to play with, and he was sending it up to the back yard right away.

"I'll have the hardware send up a little wagon soon as I can go pick one out," he said. "Every child should have a goat and wagon."

The goat was delivered promptly, a solid white goat, quite docile. Thurza came out to admire the animal. As she hung Mother's silk stockings on the clothes line, she talked to me about what fun it would be to ride in a goat-drawn wagon.

It was while we were in the kitchen, looking for an old pan to put water in for the goat, that Mr. Billy strolled down the clothesline and ate the feet out of five pairs of Mother's good stockings. Mother surveyed the damage, and almost immediately I heard her telling Daddy on the telephone, "You can cancel the delivery of that wagon. We won't be needing it." I never was exactly sure what happened to my goat.

A few days later I was in Dozier Hardware Company. Mother had gone to buy a new double boiler to cook grits in. We had grits for breakfast every morning of the world. As regularly as she brushed and braided her hair, Mother went to the kitchen at bedtime to put the grits on to soak. She measured it (our family has always contended that grits is a singular noun: grits *is*) into the top of a blue-speckled enamel boiler, covered it with water, put a top on the boiler and left it to soak overnight so it would be ready for Thurza to cook when she came to fix breakfast the next morning.

The bottom of the boiler had sprung a leak too big for a metal Fix-it to repair, so Mother was shopping for a new one. After wandering around the store, I climbed up on the sixteen foot ladder that moved past the shelves on its metal track, and Mr. Hamp Andrews gave me a ride the length of the store and back.

"Sorry about your goat," he told me. "We do have some nice wagons."

I hardly heard him. From my vantage point, high up on the ladder, I had seen a small chair, table and bookshelf, just the right size for me. They were up on the balcony at the back of the store.

As soon as Mother had made her purchase, I persuaded her to come up on the balcony with me. "You'll have to ask your Daddy," she told me. So I hurried to the bank (Mother watched me safely across the street) to tell Daddy about the furniture.

"You're too little," he told me. "Why, I bet you can't even pick the table up."

"I can, too! If I can pick up the table, will you buy it for me?"

We struck a bargain, Daddy and I, and he walked with me back to the hardware. The table was heavy (it was small—child's teaparty size—but solid oak), but I lifted it and carried it clear across the balcony. After I outgrew them, the table and chair went to a niece. I still have the book stand; it holds my collection of china and wooden rabbits.

I liked to go to Daddy's bank. It was down the street from Peoples Drug store, past Dr. White's office (I always hurried past so I wouldn't be hit by a stream of Dr. White's tobacco juice—he was a notorious spitter) and past Stanley Burge's shoe shop with its smell of leather and shoe polish. Across the alley was the Post Office, and on down the street were Dad Wynn's Barber Shop, The Hille Hotel and Dunning's Store.

The bank was an ugly brick building with wide concrete steps leading up to its double front doors. On each side of the doors, gold lettering on swinging plate glass windows identified The Farmers Bank and Trust Company. The signs said the bank closed at 2:00 P.M., but everybody knew that wasn't so. The front door might be locked at 2:00 o'clock, but the side door was open until 5:00 o'clock or later.

The last business day of the month, the bank employees worked past 11:00 P.M., getting the statements ready to mail. All of the work was done by hand, and Daddy used to say he felt as if they were working on a treadmill. Much of the sorting of checks and deposit slips was done on a long pine-top table supported by curved metal legs with the face of a Roman god molded on each one. That table now serves as my writing desk.

Daddy entered the banking business soon after he moved to Thomasville from Marengo County. He had kept books for large country stores, and he liked dealing with figures. And with people. In May, 1895, he established the Thomasville Banking Company. The birth of his first daughter, Edith, the following year so delighted him (after having two sons, he feared he was destined to have an all-male family, as his own father had done) that he had her picture put on all the bank's checks. Daddy became president of The Farmer's Bank and Trust Company when it was organized in 1907, but Edith's picture did not get on the new bank's checks.

Daddy had big eyes. "Tucker eyes," they were called. All members of his branch of the Tucker family, including me, are marked by unusually large, somewhat protruding eyes.

"We Tuckers can pick out our kinfolks by their eyes," he used to say.

Daddy's eyes were not only big, they were expressive. His every mood was reflected in his eyes: happiness, irritation, sorrow, anger, disapproval, impatience, disgust, amusement, reproof, laughter. One look from Daddy was enough to bring any unruly child into line instantly. "Bucking his eyes at you" is how my older brother described it.

His eyes aided Daddy in collecting past-due loans at the bank. On Saturday, the big trading day when nearly everybody came to town, Daddy would stand on the steps of the bank, just outside the door, and stare at the delinquent debtors as they walked along the sidewalk. Daddy wouldn't say anything, just follow the men with his eyes.

It was almost impossible to go anywhere in Thomasville without passing the bank, and even moving over to the sidewalk across the street provided no escape from Daddy's surveillance. After about two trips past the bank, the borrowers would usually come up the steps to Daddy and say,

"Mr. Tucker—about that money I borrowed. I need to talk to you."

And Daddy would reply, as pleasant as you please, "Yes, I do believe your payment is overdue. I was expecting you to stop in today so we could discuss it." Daddy's eyes looked real satisfied then.

From the time I can remember, Daddy used to say, "If you can't pay a debt, go see the person you owe the money to and explain your problem. Be honest about it. Any businessman will be patient if you show good faith." It was advice that stood me in good stead in later years when, too often, expenditures exceeded income.

Daddy had other bits of advice, of wisdom. "It's easier to get forgiveness than to get permission," he told me. However, he did not tell me this until I was nearly grown.

He advised me fairly early in life to "eat the goody and push the crusts aside." I'm not sure I understood then that he was telling me to savor the joys of life, to push aside the dulling unpleasantnesses that could detract from those joys.

Once, when I was about nine or ten years old, he gave me a lesson about snobbishness. Daddy took me with him to see a farm family out on the Tallahatta Springs Road. I entertained myself in the tire swing in the yard, twisting the rope and twirling myself around until I was dizzy, while the men talked on the porch. Then, business finished, the overalled farmer invited us to eat dinner with his family. It was my first encounter with poverty.

We washed our hands in a metal basin by the well, and we dried on a flour sack, the same sack our host's tall sons dried on when they answered his "Halloooee!!" by coming in from the field.

We ate in the corner of the kitchen, sitting on long benches at the bare table. Daddy was invited to ask the blessing. I recall that we had peas, cornbread, and a sweet, heavy pie made with plums our hostess, who never joined us at the table, had picked from a nearby thicket.

I remember that the flies, swarming in through the unscreened door and windows, were hungrier than I was. I was about to comment on the flies when I saw Daddy bucking his eyes at me. I got the same warning look when we walked through the front room where the only decorations were curling pictures, cut from old calendars, tacked to the bare walls and, on the mantelpiece, a tight bunch of sweet-shrubs in a chipped jar.

Once we were out of earshot, Daddy said, "Listen carefully. Those are honest, hardworking people. You're not a bit better than they are—you're just used to better things." I listened. And remembered.

Some of Daddy's gems of wisdom were not completely clear to me, but I understood fully what he meant when he said "You can't run with the dogs without getting fleas." He used to say that rather often when I was in my early teens and beginning to go out on dates.

Among the things it meant were that I did not go out with those "Wildcat Harrison boys" (I did go to a school party with one of those boys, and he was a perfect gentleman) and that I did not go to the Silver Slipper.

The Silver Slipper was an infamous night club on the road between Thomasville and Sunny South. A juke joint was what it was. It was a rough place where fights abounded, and drinking and gambling and goodness knows what other evil things went on. As my cousin Earl said in his newspaper column once, "The slipper may be silver, but the knuckles are brass."

Nobody "nice" went to the Silver Slipper.

One Saturday night, along about 1933, my friend, Elo Jackson, persuaded his father to let him use the family car. Mr. Jackson owned the biggest grocery store in Thomasville, so even during the Depression they had a good car and gasoline to go in it. Their car even had a radio. The radio was our major attraction this particular night.

We had made arrangements to meet some of our friends from Grove Hill, twelve miles away, at Dickinson, about halfway between the two towns. Although we never let the Thomasville boys know it, we Thomasville girls thought the Grove Hill boys were the cutest boys anywhere around. I later learned that the Thomasville boys felt the same way about the Grove Hill girls.

A gravel road connected Grove Hill and Thomasville. The only pavement was on a bridge at Dickinson, and that bridge was our rendezvous point. I'm not sure who was along that night in addition to Elo and me. Probably Helen Morgan and Neyron Nichols were with us, and maybe Ruth Williams and Mutt Wilson. We had a car full. The crew from Grove Hill likely included Massey Bedsole, Kling Harrison, Captain Coats, Fisher Ruth Tarleton, Roy Tucker and Erin Chapman.

The drivers parked on the edge of the road and we all got out. Elo turned on his car radio. For maybe an hour we listened to the music, sang along with the vocalists and danced on the bridge. There was very little traffic, almost none.

On our way home, we Thomasville residents decided to drive out past the Silver Slipper to see if we recognized any of the cars parked there. However, we found we couldn't see much just riding past, so Elo pulled up into the parking lot, off in the shadows where nobody could see us. We sat there for some time, spying on the comings and goings. It was exciting. But when we got ready to leave, Elo's car would not start. The battery was dead, dead. Patrons of the Silver Slipper came to our rescue. They, the ones who were sober enough, gathered around and pushed the car until the engine caught up.

My major concern was what Daddy would say and do when he heard, as he was sure to hear, that I had been to the Silver Slipper. There was no telling how the story would grow before it reached his ears. I decided the wisest move was to let him hear the truth from me. So as soon as Elo had escorted me safely to the door (when I first was permitted to go out with boys in cars, Daddy told me, "When you come home at night, there are three sounds I want to hear in quick succession: the car doors slam, the front steps squeak and the front door slam") I went in and waked up Daddy and told him the whole story.

"I hope your curiosity was satisfied," he said, and he turned over and went back to sleep.

I don't believe Elo fared quite as well! It was some time before Mr. Jackson let us use his car again.

Those same friends from Grove Hill, particularly those good-looking boys, were associated with one of my most embarrassing experiences. It happened the summer I was fourteen or fifteen. I had a brand new bathing suit, sent to me by Ada Gunn Dohler, a family friend who lived in New York, and I was eager to show it off. The suit was bright green, and it was made of rubber. Nobody else in Thomasville had a rubber bathing suit, and I was pretty sure nobody in Grove Hill had one either. Furthermore, it was a two-piece suit, rather daring in the early 1930s. I didn't show it to Daddy.

There was no place to swim in Thomasville. When I was younger, we used to dam up a creek in Hill's Pasture to make a swimming hole, but I had no intention of wearing my green rubber bathing suit in such a rustic, totally unsophisticated setting. I planned to wear my new suit in Grove Hill where the good-looking boys were. A landowner on the edge of Grove Hill had a pond where he let people swim. He had even built dressing rooms (we called them bath houses), and installed a pier with a diving board.

Sunday afternoon, a hot Sunday, a carload of us from Thomasville drove down to Grove Hill to go swimming. A good crowd, including the cute boys, was at the pond when we arrived. I went into the bath house to put on my suit. The other girls dressing there admired it and were properly impressed to learn that it was straight from New York and was the latest fashion.

It took a good bit of powdering and pulling to get those pants on. The top was easy: all I had to do was put my arms through the straps and tie a tight knot in the back. About four inches of my midriff was exposed! A few turns in front of the mirror assured me that I looked fine.

I walked out to the diving board with what I imagined was the poise of a New York model. I couldn't see their expressions clearly (I had left my glasses in the bath house), but I could tell that the boys were looking at me. I think Captain Coats was one of the ones who whistled. I was mighty pleased. I nodded casually to my admirers.

Then I dived into the pond. As soon as I hit the water, I realized something drastic had happened. The pants of my beautiful green rubber bathing suit had split down the back! I treaded water as long as I could, being very grateful that the pond was muddy. Then I floated on my back before I treaded some more. Finally I got the attention of my friend, Helen Morgan, and, when she swam over beside me, I whispered to her what had happened. I'll always love her for not laughing. I floated and treaded water around a bend in the pond, out of sight of everybody, where Helen brought me a towel to wrap up in. I concocted a tale about a bad headache or an attack of nausea to explain my sudden exit from the pond. The rest of the afternoon I sat on the bank and watched other swimmers in their less stylish but more reliable bathing suits.

I don't know how Daddy heard about the episode, but a day or so later he asked me, "Where's that bathing suit Ada sent you? You didn't show it to me." Then he asked, "Have you read Proverbs 16:18 recently?" His eyes were laughing. Daddy liked to laugh.

He also liked to tell stories, all sorts of stories. He nearly always had a tale to tell as we lingered over supper, a leisurely meal, but his best stories were told on our front porch on summer nights. He told stories of local history, tales about family members who lived long before I was born, absurd accounts of talking animals, his own versions of Bible stories, nonsense rhymes. Sitting in his lap or stretched out on the bench against the wall, I was sometimes puzzled by his stories, not sure whether they were true or were made up.

He used to tell about how the Tucker family came to Alabama, and I'm still not absolutely certain how much of his story is true. According to Daddy, the Tuckers, a long time ago, lived in Virginia, in a very isolated mountain community. Only one road led into the settlement, and that road was impassable much of the time. As a result, the Tuckers had very little contact with the outside world. They were backward, so backward that the only form of transportation they had ever seen were two-wheeled carts.

Well, one day a stranger came to this community, and he was driving a wagon, a four-wheeled vehicle. Everybody gathered to admire this marvel of transportation, to inspect its construction. Two of the Tucker boys—they were full grown, not youngsters—got up a bet about how long it would take the wagon's two big back wheels to catch up with its two little front wheels. So they commenced to follow the wagon. Followed it all the way to Alabama. That's how my ancestors got here. At least that's what Daddy used to say. It's the nearest we ever came to talking about genealogy.

We talked about other things, though, superstitions and local history and the folks Daddy had dealings with at the bank. He told me about Aunt Mahaley, an ancient colored woman who lived in a one-room shack perched on a red clay embankment out towards Sunny South. Only the protruding roots of an old oak tree growing beside the house kept it from tumbling down into the road.

Aunt Mahaley, who was illiterate, had a small savings account in the bank. Every few months she would walk to town with her dark green bank book in one hand and a tall staff in the other. Her snuff was in the pocket of her long apron.

"Want to see Mr. Jim," she would say to whoever happened to be at the cashier's window.

"Want to see my money," she would say to Daddy. Aunt Mahaley didn't waste words.

So Daddy, after he had looked at her bank book, would go back to the vault and get exactly the amount of money Aunt Mahaley had on deposit. Then he'd count it out slowly for her at the window.

"Thank you, Mr. Jim. I see you all are taking good care of my money." And she would take her bank book and her staff and walk home, satisfied about the safety of her earnings—for a few months.

Then there was Aunt Jenny Grayson, who lived out on the Bashi Road near the cemetery. She grew beautiful flowers in her yard. As she got older, after people began addressing her with the respectful title of "Aunt" Jenny, she found that many of her white friends would give her money on her birthday—if she reminded them when her birthday was.

She came into the bank one day with a bunch of princess feathers to give to Daddy. As she handed them to him, she said, "It's my birthday, Mr. Jim. I thought you might want to give me a little something."

"Why, Aunt Jenny," Daddy replied, "it hasn't been more than three or four months since you came in here and told me it was your birthday."

"Yes, sir. Looks like when you starts getting older, birthdays comes more often."

Daddy gave her a little something.

Daddy never told me the name of the man who came in one day and handed him a one hundred dollar bill.

"I haven't got any family, and I haven't got any friends," he told Daddy. "I've already made all the arrangements for my burial, paid for everything, but I want you to promise me to hire some people to come to my funeral."

Daddy persuaded the fellow to give the hundred dollars to a family with eight children who needed clothes and school books.

"They'll come to your funeral. And I'll see that other folks come, too," he promised.

Another of Daddy's bank friends was Mr. Jim Kelly who also belonged to the Masonic Lodge with Daddy. They were close friends. Mr. Kelly had a magnificent white beard. It was full and fluffy, the kind of beard Santa Claus would yearn for, and Mr. Kelly took good care of it, washing and combing and grooming it daily. He was mighty proud of his beard.

Well, one day when Mr. Kelly was smoking his pipe, some ashes fell on his beard and singed it rather badly. When Daddy heard about the accident, he hurried out to commiserate with Mr. Kelly about the damage to his beard.

"You know," Mr. Kelly told him, "if I hadn't been right there, my beard would have burned up!"

On another occasion, Daddy saw Mr. Kelly in the bank a day or two after his return from a Masonic conference in Montgomery, and asked, "How was the conference?"

Mr. Kelly thought for a minute before he replied, "Some I enjoyed and some I endured."

I went with Daddy to see Mr. Kelly when the old gentleman was on his death bed. He was pale and gaunt, propped up on pillows. Even his beard looked lifeless.

"Brother Tucker," he said, "it looks like my future is all behind me."

We still use that expression in our family.

Daddy did not care much about clothes. "As long as they're clean and comfortable, that's all that matters," he used to say. But he did consider well-shined shoes a mark of a gentleman. He noticed people's shoes, said you could tell a lot about a man by the shoes he wore.

One night he went downtown to watch a torchlight parade of the Ku Klux Klan. Daddy did not belong to the Klan, nor was he tolerant of its activities, but he was curious to see what size crowd the parade would attract. The father of one of my playmates was reputed to be the organizer and Grand Dragon of the Klan in Thomasville. He was a loud, officious man from North Alabama, whom Daddy disliked and mistrusted. It was in this Klansman's home (if indeed he was a member) that I first heard the word "titty" spoken by a supposedly nice lady: his wife said it right out loud! I was embarrassed and shocked.

I wanted to go with Daddy to watch the parade that night, but he wouldn't let me.

"You be careful," Mother said to him as he closed the front gate. She didn't want him to go.

We were all waiting on the front porch, rocking and not talking much, when Daddy came home.

"It was a sorry spectacle, those grown men hiding under sheets and behind masks," he reported. "I knew them every one, recognized them by their shoes. Not a decent pair of shoes in the crowd."

Though Daddy kept his shoes shined, he wore a disreputable hat much of the year. It was a Panama hat, a very expensive one given to him by a longtime friend who headed the Mexican railway system. In its day, that hat was elegant, but years of wear plus efforts by Mr. Vince McDonald to clean it (Mother was the promoter of those efforts) and between-seasons time spent in the confines of The Far Room, or hanging on the hall tree in the living room, had left it discolored, misshapen and frayed.

Every spring when Daddy swapped his winter felt for his beloved Panama, Mother entreated him to discard it and buy a new one, but Daddy paid her no attention. I was pretty sure Daddy would wear that hat to his grave, might even be buried with it.

One spring the Missionary Society of the Methodist Church was having a rummage sale, and Mother was gathering up items from around our house to donate to the project. She may have been president of the Missionary Society at the time. She frequently was.

As she walked through the living room with her box of contributions, she happened to see Daddy's Panama hat hanging on the hall tree. She stuffed it into the box, smiling a little as she did so. Then she called Thurza and asked her to take the box down to the vacant store where the sale was to be held, and give it to the chairman of the event.

An hour or two later, Daddy happened to walk past the site of the Missionary Society's sale. He glanced in the display window and saw his hat, his beloved Panama, lying there with a fifteen cent price tag on it.

Daddy bought the hat. He wore it home to dinner. Mother didn't say anything, and Daddy didn't say anything. He wore that hat at least another six or seven seasons.

There was another hat Daddy wore that his colored friend, Pete Garrett, admired and coveted. Pete used to join Daddy on our front porch on those Sunday mornings when the weather made sitting there pleasant. Daddy sat in his rocking chair, reading the Sunday *Montgomery Advertiser* and perhaps reviewing his Sunday School lesson (Daddy taught a class of men for years), and Pete sat on the top step, leaning against the bannister.

Daddy would read aloud to Pete, and they'd discuss state and local news and exchange ideas about politics. Pete couldn't read and he couldn't write, but nobody knew more about the workings of politics than Pete did. Daddy was always quoting something Pete said, some observation he made. He used to say that if Pete was just white, he'd make the finest Governor Alabama ever had.

While their conversations went on, Daddy's hat lay on the floor beside his chair, and every Sunday when Pete got up to leave, he asked Daddy to give him that hat. Every Sunday Daddy refused.

One Sunday while Daddy was asking Pete's opinion of a local politician, Pete suddenly snatched up Daddy's hat and put it on his head.

"Now you got to give me this hat," he said, grinning and backing down the steps. "I know you ain't gonna wear no hat been on a nigger's head."

I don't know what hat Daddy wore to Sunday School that day.

Whatever hat he wore, I'm sure Mother went to Sunday School and church with Daddy. So did I. I was nearly grown before I found out that some healthy, perfectly well, people did not attend Sunday services. I thought only illness with a fever above one hundred degrees served as an excuse for remaining at home.

And I hardly ate a bite the first time I sat down to a meal (I was visiting a grammar school friend) that was not blessed. I kept expecting God to strike us all dead—or at least inflict us with some loathsome illness.

I have a picture of Mother, Daddy and me on our way to Sunday School. It must have been a winter day; the trees in the background are bare. I, a solemn little two-year-old, am walking in the middle, holding my parents' hands. My Sunday dress is hidden beneath a dark (Navy blue?) coat, its velvet collar buttoned under my chin. The matching tam has a large white ribbon rosette over each ear, and I'm wearing long white stockings with white shoes.

Daddy, staring straight at the camera, has on a black suit with a white shirt and a black bow tie. His shoes are well shined, and he is wearing a hat.

Mother is wearing a dark coatsuit, her pointed-toe shoes showing beneath the long skirt. Her finger-length coat has a button trim and a narrow scarf with tassels. She is looking down at me as though she might be urging me to smile.

Even as old as I was in the picture, old enough to walk to Sunday School, my presence still surprised some people in Thomasville. Mother and Daddy had been married for twelve years when I was born, so my arrival caused a considerable stir. Daddy was fifty-two and Mother was thirty-six, both older than usual for having their first child. I do not think they had expected to have a child. Theirs was a marriage of convenience.

My mother was my father's third wife. As a young man of twenty-three, he married Miss Kate Tate, of Marengo County. Daddy was keeping books for a general mercantile store in Thomasville, and the couple lived there. Soon after the birth of their second son, his wife died.

In 1894, he married Miss Annie Long Tabb, the nineteen-year-old daughter of Edward and Harriet Newel Underwood Tabb. The account of their wedding in *The Clarke News* said, in part:

"The church was tastily decorated for the occasion with white and green by the friends of the happy couple.

"Long before the appointed hour arrived, the sacred edifice was filled to its utmost capacity with the best people of this community, friends of the bride and groom.

"Mr. Tucker is one of our leading young men and is bookkeeper for H. B. Boyles. He came to Thomasville from Marengo County and has by dint of honesty, strict attention to business, sobriety and uniform courtesy forged his way to a place in the business and social world second to none. He is in every way worthy of the hand he has won.

"The bride is one of our most popular young ladies. She grew into womanhood in this place and has friends by the score. By her sweet manners, evenness of temper and many other superior qualities of head and heart she has won a place held by few in the hearts of all who know her.

"Mr. and Mrs. Tucker received many handsome presents and telegrams of congratulations not a few."

The couple had four children: Edith, whose picture was used on the bank's checks; Ruth, who died when she was ten months old; Annelee, who could play the piano by ear almost as soon as she could walk; and Wilson, whose birth brought on his mother's death. Annie Tabb Tucker was only twenty-nine when she died.

Wilson was born, as were the other children, at home, in the two-story frame house Daddy had built on a hill (part of the ridge that was once the boundary line between the Creek and Choctaw Indians) about a mile from town. Andrew Jackson and his men, they say, camped at a spring in a ravine below the house on their way back to Tennessee after the Battle of New Orleans.

Living in that big house were Daddy and Annie and their three children; Grandfather and Grandmother Tabb; Wood and Jamie Tucker, Daddy's sons by his first marriage; Aunt Bet and her son and daughter, Jamie and Tabb Forster; and Annie's younger sister, Helen Tabb, later to be my mother. Thirteen people.

Helen Tabb, six years younger than Annie, was away from home most of the time. She went to Tuskegee to college, attending the Alabama Conference Female Institute, a Methodist-supported institution which later moved to Montgomery and was the forerunner of the present Huntingdon College. Daddy helped finance the education of his wife's sister, and he shared the pride of the family when she graduated with highest honors.

She was teaching school at Arlington, a small community some twenty miles north of Thomasville when Annie died.

Fifteen months later, she and Daddy were married. It was a simple home ceremony with all the family present, even year-old Wilson.

They were a congenial couple. They had many mutual interests, and they respected and supported each other. I never heard a cross word pass between them, never heard them fuss.

All the children loved her. They called her Heddie, her family pet name.

But Daddy's hurt, his deep grief, over the loss of his beautiful and beloved Annie never healed. His eyes brimmed with tears whenever she was mentioned, and I never heard him say her name.

Mother and Daddy's bedroom had two iron double beds in it. Mother's bed in the corner against the wall, and Daddy's between the fireplace and the windows. I slept with Mother until I was old enough—or until there was a spare room—to have a bedroom of my own. I never considered my parents' sleeping arrangement strange, not until I was much older and began to wonder about such things.

Soon after their marriage, Mother and Daddy left the two-story house on the hill and moved closer to downtown, nearer the school, into the house where I grew up.

By the time I was born, there had been many changes in the family. Grandmother and Grandfather Tabb had died. Wood Tucker had graduated from medical school and was an ear-eye-nose and throat specialist on the staff at TCI Hospital in Birmingham. Jamie Tucker was married and working as a station agent for the railroad (he later entered the veneer business at High Point, North Carolina, and became the family's only millionaire—the only child who did not attend college). Edith had graduated from Woman's College (now Huntingdon) in Montgomery and was teaching school. Jamie Forster was married, had a daughter and was living in Nashville. The household had dwindled from thirteen to six: Mother, Daddy, Annelee, Wilson, Aunt Bet and Tabb.

I was born the night Annelee graduated from high school and she never forgave me.

"Everybody was so excited about the new baby that my graduation was ignored!" she would tell me accusingly.

I was born in Selma, where the nearest hospital was located. Annie's death following childbirth made Daddy deeply concerned about Mother's welfare. He was determined that proper medical care would be available for her. Selma was sixty-five miles from Thomasville, too far to travel after labor started. So Mother rode the train to Selma in early May, 1918, and took a room at the Union Street Hospital to await my arrival. She waited nearly a month. She felt well, had no responsibilities or restrictions, and for the first time in years had leisure to read or to write letters or to nap or to be taken on outings by her Selma friends.

Many of the Selma ladies who were attentive to Mother were friends she had made through the Methodist Church, particularly the Missionary Society. Mother worked zealously for the cause of missions, and she held office at the local, district and conference levels of the Missionary Society. She devoted so much time to her mission work that I, it is told, once exclaimed, "I wish we could move to Birmingham where they don't have any Missionary Society!" I was a very little girl.

One afternoon when I was about five years old, Mother's Missionary Circle was meeting at our house. Thurza had swept and mopped and dusted and cleaned up good in the living room, and I had helped cut fresh flowers for vases (Tabb was our flower arranger) around the house and had plumped up the cushions in the chairs on the porch, making them look nice. While we were cleaning up, Mother was seeing about the refreshments. She never liked to do cleaning, never liked housework at all. My sister Edith used to say that one of her vivid recollections of Mother was seeing her hurrying to the front door to greet company, dusting with her petticoat as she went.

Cousin Golda, who was active in the Missionary Society, as well as being a piano teacher, was among the ladies engaged in mission study in the living room that afternoon. She had brought her son, Robert, a little older than I was, to play with me while the meeting was in progress. Robert was tall and slender, and he had very blond curly hair. He also had asthma.

Robert and I were playing on the porch along the ell when he suddenly flung open the door to the Far Room, shoved me into the darkness, slammed the door shut and told me, "King Tut is going to get you!"

I did not know who or what King Tut was, but I screamed with a scream that brought the entire Missionary Circle out of the living room and down the porch to my rescue.

By the time they reached me, Robert had already run around the corner by the church, on his way home to hide.

It took a good little while for me and the Missionary Circle to calm down enough so I could pass the napkins and they could have refreshments. The group dispensed with whatever program they were having that King Tut afternoon.

It was also Robert who provoked me to one of my few displays of violence. I was a little older then, not much, and once again the Missionary Circle was meeting with Mother and once again Cousin Golda had brought Robert to play with me. We were in the kitchen, Robert and I, and there was a fire in the wood stove. Robert put some water in a pan, added a handful of chicken feed, what we called chops, put the pan on the stove and began to stir.

"I'm making whiskey," he told me.

I watched in shock and disbelief as the baking soda he then stirred into the mixture began to fizz.

"Stop!" I shouted. I beat on him with my fists and began to

kick him. Whiskey in my Mother's kitchen? And the Missionary ladies meeting under the same roof? Never! My outburst and my forceful defense of the sanctity of my Mother's kitchen so surprised Robert that he abandoned his project and fled.

Robert's father had some fine hunting hounds. There were reports that when Robert needed money, he would let the dogs out of their pens so he could later claim a reward for finding then and returning them safely. I'm not sure whether that's true or not. Could be.

That picture of Mother, Daddy and me on our way to church is one of the few pictures I have of Mother. There's a tintype of her as a little girl, but it had faded so that the features are barely distinguishable.

My favorite is a picture of her taken by a traveling photographer when she was sixteen. It shows a pensive, unsmiling young girl sitting on the porch steps playing—or holding—a guitar. Her hair is in stiff curling-iron waves and is held by a bow in the back. She is sitting on a rug, a patterned runner, put on the steps to protect her white dress, a dress with lace and frills.

A thick growth of morning glory vines, climbing up over the bannisters to shade the porch, provides a leafy background. I don't know what chord she is fingering, and I wonder if she knew. I didn't know she played the guitar, not until I found the photograph in an old trunk. When I asked about it, she laughingly replied, "O, I could play 'The Spanish Fandango'—that's all!"

Kodaks and Hill's Pasture

I DON'T BELIEVE I ever took a picture of Mother, which seems strange; photography was one of my hobbies.

I got my first camera in 1930, the summer I was twelve. Eastman Kodak was observing its fiftieth (golden) anniversary that year, and part of the celebration centered around giving box cameras to boys and girls born in 1918. Each Kodak dealer had a limited number of Brownies to give away.

Peoples Drug Store, right on the corner in downtown Thomasville, was the authorized Kodak dealer for our area. Mr. Theodore Megginson, the owner, put a sign in the window telling about the free cameras. I stopped and read that sign every time I walked past the drug store.

On the appointed day, I was the first child in line. I sat on the edge of the high sidewalk there on the drug store corner and watched the sun come up. The second child to arrive that morning was Boolie Cogle, from Dixon's Mills. Boolie didn't really need a free camera; his daddy could have bought Eastman Kodak Company if he had wanted to, but maybe he didn't want to spend money on a camera for Boolie.

Mr. Cogle came to southwest Alabama from Virginia (he always pronounced "house" and "about" in a way that folks could tell he didn't grow up in the piney woods), borrowed some money from Daddy's bank, and began to buy timber land. He got to be one of the largest landowners, biggest sawmill operators and richest men in our part of the state, but just to look at him, nobody would ever guess it.

He and Mrs. Cogle had eight children. Mr. Cogle always said

he wanted to make enough money to leave a million dollars to each of his children. He was proud of his big family, and every time a new baby was born he'd blow the whistle at his mill long and loud.

That mill whistle also served as Thomasville's fire alarm. Sometimes its blasts were confusing; folks couldn't tell whether the mill whistle was summoning the volunteer firemen or announcing the birth of a new Cogle.

They were an unpretentious family, lived simply in their big country home. On one occasion, Mr. Cogle took several of his children with him to Mobile to show them the sights of the port city. He was wearing his logging clothes, and the children were all barefooted. As they walked through Bienville Square, a kindly gentleman stopped Mr. Cogle and asked, "Are all these children yours?"

"Yes, sir," Mr. Cogle replied.

"Here," said the gentleman, thrusting a five dollar bill in Mr. Cogle's hand, "This will help you buy them some shoes."

Mr. Cogle thanked the benefactor and put the money, carefully folded, into his pocket.

One morning when Mr. Cogle was going to Montgomery on business, Mrs. Cogle said to him, "Bruce, you go to Montgomery often, and not a one of our children has ever seen the capitol. I think that's a shame."

"Well, I guess it is," Mr. Cogle agreed. "You get as many of them ready as you can, and I'll take them with me today."

So Mrs. Cogle got a car full of children dressed and ready and Mr. Cogle drove them to Montgomery. It took a long time to drive from Dixon's Mills to Montgomery back then, but the Cogle children were well-behaved and didn't give their daddy a bit of trouble. When they got to Montgomery, Mr. Cogle had some business to see about before he could take his children sight-seeing, so he took them to the Exchange Hotel, rented a room and instructed them to wait quietly until he returned.

"I'll show you lots of things—the Capitol, the first White

House of the Confederacy, Court Square fountain—lots of things. We may even ride on the streetcar and eat at the Elite," he promised.

It was late, and Mrs. Cogle was beginning to get uneasy when Mr. Cogle drove into the yard that night. She must have looked out the window a dozen times, hoping to see his headlights, before she heard him drive up. She hurried out to welcome her weary brood. Only Mr. Cogle got out of the car.

"Bruce! Where are the children?"

"O, Lord! I forgot all about them! They're in the hotel room in Montgomery!"

Tired as he was, he had to turn around and go back to Montgomery, two hundred and thirty miles round trip, and get his children.

I don't know whether or not they ever got to go to Montgomery again, but if they did, I'm sure Boolie took a picture of the Capitol with his Brownie.

Those commemorative Brownies were tan with a gold seal on the side. I don't know what happened to mine, but I took lots of pictures with it.

Some Sunday afternoons we went Kodaking, a whole bunch of us, to Hill's Pasture, just east of town beyond Evelyn and Teace's house and Huey, Curtis, Margaret and Edwin Ford's house. They were cousins, and we all played together. Huey had a pony named Jiggs, who occasionally posed for our pictures.

One Sunday after the benediction at church, I was asking Mother's permission to go Kodaking in Hill's Pasture. A woman listening to our conversation said, "O, Helen, let her go. I'm sure they won't do anything ugly in God's beautiful woods."

We, in our innocence, had never thought of "doing anything ugly." I wanted to kick that woman. I wish I had.

Among the pictures I made with my Brownie in Hill's Pasture was one of Evelyn and Teace in front of the log cabin we built. It took us all one summer to build that cabin. First we had to find a safe location, somewhere Preston McCrary and his gang could never find. Preston was the Baptist preacher's son.

The spot we selected was a wooded cove just beyond First Crossing. Here the path crossed the creek, narrow enough to jump across most of the year. It was here at First Crossing that we built our dams (no dam ever lasted an entire season) to create our swimming hole each summer.

At Rock Bottom, about a quarter of a mile further in the pasture, the creek twisted around big boulders, worn into strange shapes by centuries of running water. Along its banks, in the softer soapstone, we dug out shells and fossils millions of years old. We, in our twelve-year old wisdom, argued over how long it had been since the sea covered the spot where we stood. I got an early lesson in creationism vs. evolution.

When I asked Mother, she said, "It makes no difference whether those fossils are four thousand years old or four million. God created a marvelous world, no matter when He did it, or how long He took."

Mother delighted in God's creations. One night, one August night when the meteorologists had predicted showers of meteors, Mother put a mattress—or had it put—on the roofless part of our back porch. I slept out there on the porch with her that night.

Mother nudged me awake when the stars began racing across the sky. "Look! Look!" We lay there in the darkness, Mother and I, watching the display. Those stars scooted and scattered in the night, like the glowing ashes flipped from the cigars Daddy sometimes smoked, like the sparklers Santa Claus left in my stocking.

"The heavens declare the glory of God; and the firmament showeth His handiwork," Mother said. I could tell by the reverence in her voice that she was quoting the Bible, but I did not recognize the nineteenth Psalm. I only knew the words were beautiful. Later I learned that Psalm, just as I learned other Psalms and passages from the Bible, and words to hymns (all verses!) on Sunday afternoons.

I brought a handful of shell fossils from Rock Bottom to Mother one day. She spread them out on the corner of the kitchen table, then gently picked them up, one at a time, as she recited: "The earth is the Lord's, and the fullness thereof; the world and they that dwell therein. For He hath founded it upon the seas, and established it upon the floods." I later learned that Psalm, Psalm Twenty-four, too.

We built our cabin between those two crossings. It was made of poplar logs, notched to fit together, and it had openings for a low door and two windows on the front. It was roofed with sheets of rusty metal from the Fords' barn.

Getting that roofing to our building site was the most difficult phase of our project. Lookouts had to be posted all along our route to make sure Preston's gang members did not see us toting the metal sheets (we carried them on our heads) to our secret cove.

We got our roof finished, and we chinked the cracks between the logs with a mixture of moss and mud. Our final building plans called for putting a door in the entrance (we had a padlock and key ready to use) and covering the windows with shades of some kind, but we never got to carry out those plans.

One day we found our cabin in ruins: roof torn off, logs pulled apart and scattered all up and down the cove. Our rivals had done a thorough job of destroying it. But summer was nearly over. School would be starting soon. And the fun had been in the building.

Once, while we were working on the cabin, Evelyn and I were dispatched to her house to get nails or a hammer, or maybe a jug of water. We had almost reached First Crossing when one of Mr. Hill's bulls came charging toward us.

Evelyn ran for a pine tree, and I headed for a tree right beside it. We had often climbed young pine trees to their tops, so high that our weight bent them over and we rode them to the ground. It was a different kind of climbing we did that day!

Once we were safely out of reach of his horns, we looked down at our adversary. That bull was angry, very angry. He pawed the ground, sending clumps of yellow bitterweeds flying, and he snorted and circled the trees we had climbed.

(Perhaps I should not interrupt the tale at this point, but it needs to be understood that Evelyn and I did not think of the

I was about four years old when I posed with muff and corduroy coat for Mr. Rich Anderson in his studio.

My paternal grandparents, the Rev. and Mrs. James Lee Tucker

My mother, Helen Tabb Tucker, at age sixteen with her guitar on the steps of her home and, *right*, as a young lady, perhaps when she graduated from the Alabama Conference Female College or when she was a bride.

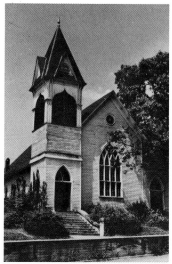

Mother, Daddy, and I on our way to Sunday School at the Methodist Church, shown at right and now demolished

Aunt Bet with the cake she made for my wedding

Daddy, with our dog Sikes leading the way, going back to his office after dinner (noon) about 1932. Their route always took them through the lumber yard.

Bill Ryan and me astride a log in the lumber yard in the late 1920s

A Tom Thumb wedding in Thomasville in the early 1920s. I am the bridesmaid with the huge bow in her hair (third from right)

Tying luggage to the outside of the car in preparation for a family trip in the summer of 1933 are, left to right, Aunt Bet, Tabb, Spurgeon Hill (he often drove for us), Thurza (squatting), Annelee, and Mother

It actually ran, this car that belonged to Gerald Lowery. Behind the wheel is Ruth Williams, who learned to drive about the time she started to school and who drove everywhere when she was twelve. I am sitting beside her in this 1934 photograph.

Bill Ryan and Osceola Green with me at a homecoming at Bethel Church in the 1930s. Osceola was—and is—the favorite piano player in south Alabama. She was playing for the singing that Sunday.

For two football seasons, 1933 and 1934, I was a cheer-leader for the Thomasville High School football team. One of the players was Lyles Carter Walker, shown here, standing on our front porch steps, wearing his football sweater.

This summer day I was swimming with the Dumas family (I am second from right) at a "wash hole" dubbed Caney Head. This was in the late 1920s—before the rubber bathing suit.

Thomasville High School's senior class outing at Beck's Landing on the Alabama River in 1935. Left to right are my friend Ruth Williams, Tom Hadley Tyson (Robert's older brother—not a member of our graduating class), and me.

animal as a bull. Certainly we never said the word. A male cow was, in our sheltered world, called a beast, or a BB. At our house, when Thurza fried chicken, we never had legs or thighs; those pieces were drumsticks and second joints. Our chickens did have breasts, however.)

So there we were, Evelyn and I, treed by the bellowing BB! We knew nobody could hear our cries of distress, so we didn't holler for help. We just clung to the trees and hoped we could hold on until we were rescued.

"It'll be hours before anybody comes," Evelyn said. She began to sob. I might have cried, too, but crying got my glasses all smudged up, and I didn't have anything to wipe them on. And I couldn't turn loose to take them off and wipe them, even if I'd had wiping material. So I didn't cry.

"Huey and Curtis and Lyles Carter and them won't come for hours, not until the 11:30 mill whistle blows," Evelyn said. "No telling how long that will be." She cried some more.

We could only guess at the passage of time. No child we knew had a wrist watch. The only watches I'd ever had were the play-like ones Cousin Tabb stamped on my wrist with the round, red postmark at the Post Office. Tabb gave every little child who came into the Post Office one of those watches. Normally, we needed no timepieces. Our lives were regulated by the blowing of the mill whistle and the arrivals of the trains.

I was trying to think of words of encouragement and fortitude to say to Evelyn when, off in the distance, I saw Preston and his gang approaching. I was glad I had not cried and smudged up my glasses.

"Look, Evelyn! Yonder come Preston and them! Maybe they'll chase the BB away."

I watched the boys, five or six of them, spot us up in the trees, saw them eye the BB (they probably just came right out and said "bull"). They gathered up rocks and sticks and ran toward the animal, shouting and chunking as they ran. The BB turned toward them, changed his mind and went thundering off toward First Crossing with Preston and his cohorts right behind him.

Those boys never even looked up at us as they ran past. They did stop at the edge of the clearing, though, and turn and laugh at us. They yelled something at us, too, that I'm not sure I understood. The whole episode was very humiliating. I'm glad nobody took a picture of Evelyn and me and the BB.

Mr. Rich Anderson developed and printed the pictures I took. His first name was not a descriptive adjective—his name was Richard. Other men in our town did have descriptive first names: Mr. Mule Morgan, who traded mules and horses (and made a fortune); Mr. Chicken Bouler, who drove all over the county buying chickens to sell when the chicken car parked on the railroad sidetrack; and Mr. Watch Anderson, a kinsman of Mr. Rich, who repaired watches in his jewelry store. A customer wrote him once, "I heard you was dead. If you is, that's all right. If you ain't, please let me know when I can come get my watch."

Then there was Mr. One-Eyed Billy Wilson, who had a room at the White Hotel down by the railroad tracks. Whenever the preacher talked about the "all-seeing eye of God" or I saw God's eye in a stained glass window, I always thought of little old, dried-up Mr. One-Eyed Billy Wilson. I tried not to ever let him look at me.

Miss Julia White, who ran the White Hotel, was always trying to marry Mr. One-Eyed Billy Wilson off to somebody, but she never had any luck. Miss Julia's husband, Mr. Dave White, died from sitting on top of an open barrel of chemicals used to dip cattle in. They say the fumes "entered his body" and killed him. I remember watching men drive herds of cattle past our house on their way to the dipping vat, and every time I saw them, I thought about Mr. Dave White. Mr. Dave White, before his unfortunate accident, used to hang the bleached skulls of animals on the fence posts around his field.

Before I was born, there was a swimming pool behind the White Hotel. The concrete walls were still there when I was a little girl. One day, after I had been visiting my friend, Mrs. Rebecca Moseley at the White Hotel (Mrs. Moseley gave me a blue and white milk glass hen dish she had planned to have put on her grave), I asked Miss Julia White about cleaning out the swimming pool and using it again.

"Can't," she answered. "For years we've been throwing the feathers from the chickens we dress over into that old dry pool. We serve chicken nearly every day here at the hotel. So many feathers in there you never would get it cleaned out." I never did get to go behind the hotel and look over the wall to see if she was telling the truth.

As I was saying, Mr. Rich Anderson owned and operated the only photographic studio in Thomasville. His studio (he called it his shop) was in the back of Leo Moore's barber shop, right by the town ditch. In a large room with a northern skylight were his black-draped camera on its wooden tripod, an oblong sink for washing his prints, a long row of cluttered pigeonholes, and a wobbly piano stool on which all his subjects posed. Behind the stool hung a scenic backdrop, the trademark of an Anderson photograph. This background, a greyish painting of the distant seas seen through Corinthian columns and flower-bedecked balustrades, never changed except to become more faded and more dusty.

A black comb dangled from a string beside a cracked mirror over the sink. The comb and mirror were the only concessions Mr. Anderson made to his patrons' vanity. He did not believe in using makeup, in flattering lighting, or in re-touching negatives.

"If folks don't want to know how they really look, they ought not to have their pictures made. A picture is even more honest than a mirror," he used to say. Mr. Anderson did not have many female customers.

He himself would never be called handsome. His eyebrows were thick and bristly, like his hair, and he nearly always needed a shave. His square hands, stained by chemicals, were the color of the tobacco juice he spit into the box of sand beside his camera. His heavy shoulders were stooped and his head was thrust so far forward that he barely had to change his stance when he covered his head and shoulders with black cloth and peered into his camera.

Mr. Anderson was not a man to hurry. He believed in taking his time, whether he was setting out collards in his garden or photographing a team of restless football players. He delayed the departure of many a newly-married couple by his refusal to rush through the ritual of taking wedding pictures, and there's no telling how much ice cream melted at birthday parties while he methodically arranged the uncooperative guests and honoree for a picture.

The only time Mr. Anderson ever got in a hurry was the day Mr. Tom Butler burst into his shop and shouted, "I want a picture of my wife!"

Mr. Anderson was washing a batch of prints in the sink, and he aimed to finish the job before he answered, the way he usually did when anyone interrupted him. But the tone of Mr. Butler's voice made him dry his hands on the seat of his pants and turn around to his customer.

"What did you want? A picture of your wife? If you'll just look through that stack of negatives over there in the corner, I believe you'll find one of her."

The stack of negatives was maybe four feet high. In fact, there were two stacks of negatives leaning against each other there in the corner. Mr. Anderson was not orderly.

"Find it yourself! Right now!" Mr. Butler snapped.

Mr. Anderson got in a hurry for one of the few times in his life. But though he hurried, it took him more than an hour to find the negative. All the time he looked, he kept promising himself that he was going to file those negatives in alphabetical order, and he kept wondering why Mr. Butler was so eager to have a picture of his wife. They did not appear to be an especially affectionate couple.

The negative showed Mrs. Butler being installed as an officer in a garden club or a church group. Mr. Anderson couldn't remember which. He made an eight by ten print of the negative, the fastest printing he'd ever done, and he was so relieved to hand it over to Mr. Butler that he forgot to collect for it.

A couple of days later, Mr. Anderson's curiosity was satisfied:

trees and fences and barns and telephone poles all over the countryside were plastered with handbills offering a reward of $100.00 for information leading to the return of Mrs. Butler. Her picture was right there on each one.

The handbills didn't say so, but Mrs. Butler had run off with a traveling hardware salesman. They did give a complete description of her, including a jagged scar on her left thigh. The picture didn't show that, of course.

The errant wife returned home a few days later. They say she claimed the $100.00 reward—and got it! She was angry, they said, with Mr. Butler for putting her picture on public display (she disliked the photograph, thought it unflattering), but his having described her as weighing ten pounds more than she actually did is what upset her most.

I don't know who told me about the Butlers. I'm sure I did not hear it at home; my ears were protected from such gossip. As soon as grown-ups began gossiping, I was always told, "Kathryn, please go feed the chickens." I was thus banished before I could hear anything of interest. The summer a leading singer in our choir ran off with the area's best bootlegger, we had the fattest chickens in the whole country!

Laps and Rocking Chairs

THERE WAS ALWAYS a lap to sit in. Whether I needed comfort or entertainment or the quiet affirmation of love, there was always a lap.

Our house abounded in rocking chairs. There were the big green rockers on the porch; a low rocker, handmade of applewood, that came from Virginia with Mother's family; a heavy oak rocker upholstered in black leather that Aunt Bet won for entering the best cake in the county fair; a small, armless rocker "just right for rocking babies"; a sturdy rocker with wide arms, Daddy's favorite to sit in by the fire; and others. Only the kitchen and dining room lacked rocking chairs. Thurza did not need a rocking chair in the kitchen. On those rare occasions when she sat down, she could lean back in her straight chair, balance on its back legs, and rock as smoothly as if she were sitting in Daddy's chair.

One morning she did sit in Daddy's chair. She rocked me there. I was about three years old. I had a dog named Pete, a beautiful, gentle Scotch collie, that I loved very much. Actually, Pete was my brother Wilson's dog, but since Wilson (he was thirteen years older than I) was gone nearly all day, Pete thought he belonged to me. So did I.

I remember one day Wilson put Pete on the wide shelf by our well, climbed up beside him, and then lifted the dog up to the flat part of our back porch roof. He did the same thing with me. Then the three of us, Pete, Wilson and I, climbed up the sloping shingle roof to the high ridge pole where we walked slowly back and forth, balancing carefully. Daddy happened to come outside the bank. He looked across the vacant lots, across the railroad track, across the lumber yard and saw us on top of the house, silhouetted against the sky. He hurried to the telephone to call Mother. "Where's Kathryn?" he asked. "Out in the backyard playing with Wilson," Mother replied. "You'd better go see. Quick!" Daddy told her. Mother nearly had a spasm, what we call in our family "a committee fit," when she saw us on top of the house.

Back to Thurza and the rocking chair.

Pete had been sick for several days. He was tied to the fig tree on the edge of the yard, where it was shady all day, and I was instructed not to go near him. He had sore mouth (canine pellagra), Daddy told me. Ben Burroughs, who took care of Mr. Alex Gunn's hunting dogs, came every day and fed Pete sardines and rubbed his mouth with the oil from the can. Even when Ben fed him and talked to him and rubbed him, Pete just lay there under the fig tree, hardly moved at all.

One morning when I waked up, everybody had left the house except Thurza who was washing dishes in the kitchen. I could hear her singing there. Just as I walked out on the porch to go to the kitchen, I saw Ben dragging Pete, stiff in death, across the backyard.

Thurza heard my first cry. She grabbed me up in her arms and sat down with me in Daddy's chair. She didn't say anything, just held me and patted me and rocked me and let me cry. When Mother came in, Thurza handed me to her and said simply, "She seen Ben hauling Pete off. She gonna need some extra petting for awhile."

Mother was such a small woman that I outgrew her lap early. When I, long-legged and angular, no longer fit comfortably in her lap, she made a space for me beside her in her chair so we could rock while she read to me or told me stories and sang. The only song I remember her singing was "Sweet Marie," an old love song: "Come to me, Sweet Marie / Sweet Marie, come to me / Not because your face is fair / Love, to see / But your soul so pure and sweet / Makes my happiness complete / Makes me falter at your feet, Sweet Marie".

Every week Mother read me stories from the children's page in "The Christian Observer," the Presbyterian Church paper she subscribed to until her death. Those stories were always very moral, upright. I liked it better when Tabb read me Uncle Wiggley stories about Nurse Jane Fuzzy Wuzzy and the Pipsisewah and the Skeezix. Mother also taught me The Child's Catechism while we rocked together. I was too big to fit in the chair with her when I memorized The Shorter Catechism.

Aunt Bet had an ample lap, but she seldom sat down. When she did sit, she usually had peas to shell or pecans to pick out or handwork to finish. It was she who sang the greatest variety of songs:

> My Master's got a brand new house,
> It's sixteen stories high,
> And every room in that big house
> Is filled with chicken pie.
>   Bye-O-bye, Miss Dolcy,
>   Sleep to the rattle of the bow.
>   Slumber 'til morning,
>   I love Miss Dolcy so.
> If I had a needle and thread
> As fine as I could sew,
> I'd sew Miss Dolcy to my side
> And take her to Baltimo'.

and

> Prettiest little gal I ever did know,
> Prettiest little gal in the county-o.
> Mama and Papa told me so.
> Looked in the glass and found it so.

and

> Chicken in the bread tray
> Scratching in the dough.
> Granny, will your dog bite?
> No, child, no.

She knew all the verses to "Billy Boy" and "Frog Went

a'Courtin'." Sometimes she sang sad songs such as "Where Is My Wandering Boy Tonight?" and "After The Ball," and "The Soldier's Farewell."

Tabb favored sprightlier songs when she rocked and sang to me: "Yes, We Have No Bananas," "I'm Forever Blowing Bubbles" and "Wait 'Til The Sun Shines, Nellie" and such. My favorite was a nonsense song that went something like:

Johnny Boy, who cut your hair?
You say your mother did?
Did she cut it with a meat ax,
You funny looking kid?
Did she freeze it, boy, and break it off?
Whatever she did was wrong!
So take my advice,
If you want to look nice,
And, Johnny, let your hair grow long!

Tabb rocked vigorously while she held me and sang. It was fun. Sometimes we'd laugh so hard I'd roll out of her lap and she'd lose her breath and couldn't sing any more.

It was Tabb who made a game of "This Little Piggy Went To Market" so exciting I wanted to play long past babyhood, and it was Tabb who played William Trimbletoe and Club Fist and Jack-in-the-Bush with me.

"Measles" was an entertainment she concocted for me. Holding a lighted candle, she tilted it so that drops of wax fell on her outstretched hand and arm. After the "measle spots" hardened, we peeled each one off very gently. Then it would be my turn to have measles and Tabb, being very careful not to let the melted wax burn, would speckle my arms and legs. If we could find red or green candles left over from Christmas, we had colored measles spots, but most of the time we contented ourselves with the white ones.

Sometimes I sat in her lap so Tabb could get splinters out of my bare feet. She had the best eyes in the family and could see to ease a splinter or a sticker out so that it hardly hurt at all. She could even see redbugs. Not many people could see those tiny red pests that burrowed into the skin and raised itchy, red welts, but Tabb could see them and get rid of them.

Tabb doctored many of my hurts. After she had removed the splinter (sometimes we had to wait a day or two so it could fester before she could get it out) or gotten rid of the red bugs or squeezed a rising (I still call it a "rison") I wouldn't let anybody else touch, she poured hydrogen peroxide on the places. It, the antiseptic, was a clear liquid that came in a dark brown bottle. The more it fizzed, the more germs it was killing, Tabb said. I liked to watch it fizz.

When I sat in Daddy's lap, out on the porch on summer nights, he smelled of tobacco, and the starch Thurza used in his shirt. Sometimes he put his pipe aside and smoked a cigar.

"You like music," he would say to me. "I'm going to give you a whole band," and he would slide the band off his cigar and put it on my thumb.

Daddy sang to me, too:

Where, O, where has my little dog gone?
Where, O, where can he be?
With his tail cut short
And his ears cut long,
O, Where, O, where can he be?

And, my favorite, The Mosquito Song:

Buzz, buzz, buzz!
There's someone in this bed.
Buzz, buzz, buzz!
No hair upon his head.
Buzz, buzz, buzz!
We'll paint old baldhead red.
There'll be a hot time
In the old town tonight!

Daddy pretended to be swatting mosquitoes off his bald head while he sang.

Wilson

I DON'T THINK I ever sat in Wilson's lap, except when he let me "help" him drive the car. I adored my big brother, wanted to do whatever he was doing and go wherever he went. They say when I was a baby, fretful and cross, I'd be all smiles as soon as Wilson came close enough for me to touch him. Later, when I was a year or so old, he wired a box (I think it was a wooden shell crate) to the back fender of his bicycle so he could ride me around town. I don't remember that.

I do remember how he used to let me dance with him. He would wind up the Victrola, put on "My Blue Heaven" or "Yes, Sir, That's My Baby," and let me stand on his feet while he danced me around and around the living room. He was a graceful, smooth dancer, had the reputation for being the best dancer in six counties, though nobody ever named for me which six.

He excelled at playing basketball, was the finest baseball pitcher our school ever had, was an elusive, if skinny, fullback on the football team, and was an expert rifle shot years before he put on long pants. When Wilson was dancing, or striking out a batter, or scoring a touchdown, people forgot how badly he stuttered. And so did he.

Wilson and his friends, when they were in high school in the early 1920s, liked to go to the dances in Camden, across the Alabama River about thirty miles away. Wilson's bedroom was on the ell at our house so, if he tiptoed past Aunt Bet and Tabb's room, nobody ever knew how late he came home. He did have one restriction: he had to get back in time to sweep out the bank before it opened—and Daddy opened the bank early.

No bridge spanned the river, so the crossing was made on a

wooden ferry boat, at Holly's Ferry. The ferryman and his family lived in a small house atop a bluff on the Camden side of the river.

One night, after Wilson and his cronies had danced long past midnight, the ferryman refused to take them back across the river, said the river was high and the crossing would be too dangerous in the dark. No matter how they pleaded or what promises they made (they did not have enough money among them to make an attractive offer), the ferryman would not change his mind. He said he was going to sleep until daylight and suggested that they stretch out on his porch and do the same.

Wilson knew he had to be back in Thomasville by daylight so he could sweep out the bank. He may have heard the story about his Grandfather Tucker swimming the Tombigbee River, but that feat was accomplished in the daytime. Wilson was not about to try to swim the Alabama River in the dark!

What that crew did was roll two empty metal oil drums up under the ferryman's window and beat on those drums with tire tools until the ferryman, despairing of getting any sleep, agreed to take them across the river.

Wilson was just finishing his sweeping when Daddy got to the bank.

Wilson had another upsetting experience at Holly's Ferry, this one in the daytime, when he went there to meet my sister, Edith, and bring her and her young son to Thomasville for a visit. Sister (Edith) and her family lived in Greenville. When there was visiting back and forth, we would meet at the river, about half way between Thomasville and Greenville, and swap passengers and baggage at the ferry there.

Sister wrote that she wanted to bring her little boy, William Halsell Ryan, Jr. (Bill), for a visit, so Wilson, the best driver in the family, was dispatched to meet them at Holly's Ferry. After the plans were all made, the weather turned bad. It rained enough to make those unpaved, ungraveled roads both slick and sticky. The steep inclines leading down to the river were hazardous, particularly the one on the west bank, our side of the Alabama.

Wilson had learned to drive on such roads, and he was confident he could make the trip safely. It was still raining when he got to the river. He stopped at the top of the bluff, being careful to stay in the ruts, and waited for his passengers to arrive on the other side. He figured he would have to wait: the Ryans had a reputation for being late. (Will Ryan was ten minutes late for his wedding when he married Sister—stopped on the way to get a shoe shine. Their wedding in our home is one of my earliest memories, principally because I was not allowed to be in it.)

When the car from Greenville did arrive, Wilson eased down the steep grade while the ferry made its crossing. He had turned around (no easy feat!) and was headed up the hill toward home by the time the ferryman guided the rickety craft to the landing. The rain was still falling.

Wilson put Sister's suitcases into the car and checked again to make sure the side curtains were all securely fastened.

When he looked around, Sister was sloshing up the hill, holding Bill (he was swaddled in layers of wrappings to protect him from the weather) in one arm and an umbrella in her other hand.

No matter how hard Wilson begged and pleaded, Sister would not get into the car, just kept trudging through the mud with Wilson driving real slow beside her and urging her to get in. She wasn't, she said, going to risk her baby's life to Wilson's driving on that slick road.

In later years, Wilson said Sister walked a mile or two in the rain and mud with her baby in her arms before he coaxed her into the car, but he was probably exaggerating. He did that.

I crossed that river many times as a child and as a teen-ager going for summer visits with Sister, Will, Bill and Jim, the little brother seven years Bill's junior. Will owned a drug store, Ryan Drug Company, where I could have a chocolate ice cream soda free every day and could choose an assortment of magazines from the rack in the store to take to their house to read (years later a woman in Greenville told me, "When my boy was in prison, your sister sent him magazines to read every single month. I'll never forget that—and he won't either."), and where they had the cutest soda jerker I ever saw, a boy named Poodle Pierce. There was a library where I could check out books and, not too far from town, an icy pool to swim in. I saw my first talking movie in Greenville, and Sister bought me my first pair of silk stockings there. I wore them to a party at the Beelands' house. I checked every few minutes to make sure my seams were straight. Sister made teen-agers welcome at her house, liked to have informal gatherings (shindigs, we called them) there. One night after a shindig, after Bill and Jim were fast asleep, I walked into the living room and found Sister and Will dancing to the music of their wind-up Victrola. They were never aware of my presence, but I'll never forget how romantic, graceful, happy—and young—they were dancing there. If I had told Wilson about it, he would have said he taught Sister to dance.

As I said, Wilson was an expert shot, fine dancer and an excellent hunter. The first letter he printed to Santa Claus (preserved in the family archives) asked only for a box of shells. It was signed "Your customer, Wilson." Aunt Bet must have helped him spell customer.

I admired Wilson's hunting prowess, just as I admired everything he did and I longed to be big enough to go hunting with him. One day, when I was about four years old, Wilson saw a baby bird, not quite able to fly, perched near the ground on the wire fence that enclosed our chicken yard. The bird was perfectly framed in one of the small wire hexagons.

"How would you like to shoot a bird?" Wilson asked me.

Even before I could answer, he had gone to his room to get his air rifle. He stooped down beside me, handed me the gun, aimed it at the little bird, and told me, "Pull the trigger."

I did. The bird fell over dead. I had shot a bird! I was about to run to the kitchen to tell Thurza about my accomplishment when Wilson said to me:

"Just look what you have done. You've killed this poor little bird. He never will get to see his mama again. I expect she's at home now, waiting for him and wondering where her little baby bird is. And you've killed him."

I cried and I cried and I cried.

Perhaps that's why when I was old enough to have my own air rifle, I never shot birds. I used my BB shots to puncture Calumet Baking Powder cans set up in a row on our back fence. And I could hit Chief Calumet on those cans almost as dead center as Wilson could.

Wilson took cruel delight in teasing me. "Well," he'd say, "I'm tired of living. I'm going to hold my breath and stop breathing and die. I'm not ever going to breathe any more."

I'd cry and beg him to breathe. After what seemed forever, he would draw a deep breath as he reassured me, "Well, if you want me to, I'll breathe again." No matter how many times he put on this not-going-to-breathe-anymore act, I reacted in the same dumb way.

I also cried and begged on those occasions when Wilson threatened me with starvation. We'd hear the dinner bell ring, summoning the family to the dining room, and he would grab my arms and hold fast to my wrists so I could not pull away.

"You hear that bell? I'm not going to let you go eat. You'll just starve to death. They'll come looking for you, and all they'll find will be a little pile of bones," Wilson would tell me.

But the threat that lingered longest, that still comes plummeting out of the past on sleepless nights, was his muttered, "I'm going to jerk off your leg and beat you over your head with the bloody end."

Although he teased me and made me cry, it was also Wilson who made kites for me and helped me fly them, who taught me to play marbles and to shoot a slingshot, showed me how to pick out "Chopsticks" on the piano, carved baskets out of peach seeds for me, and brought me pocketsful of chinquapins from the woods. He tried to teach me how to wiggle my ears, but I never mastered that art.

Barber Shops

EVERYBODY IN TOWN knew how much I loved Wilson, and some folks, especially in the barber shop, delighted in teasing me about him. I'd be sitting on the board across the arms of Mr. Luther Moore's barber chair, with his blue-striped cotton cape draped around me, and someone would ask, "Are you Billy Tucker's sister?" Nearly everyone called him Billy.

"His name is not Billy. It's Wilson," I would reply.

"Wilson. Well, I don't blame him for changing his name. If I was as sorry as he is, I'd change my name, too."

"He's not sorry! He's good!!" I'd yell, tears of anger welling in my eyes.

"You all talking about that old sorry Billy Tucker?" another man, his voice muffled by the steaming towel folded around his face, would ask.

"He's not sorry! He's not sorry!!"

Then when they sensed I could bear their teasing no longer, my tormentors would suddenly begin to talk about the baseball games they'd seen Wilson pitch (they still called him Billy, but they left out the "sorry"), bragging on his athletic ability, and I would be placated. I'd be calm enough to sit still so Mr. Moore could trim my bangs.

I think I was the only little girl in Thomasville who went to the barber shop. I not only got my hair cut there among all those teasing men, I also got my hair shampooed.

There wasn't a beauty parlor in Thomasville then, and washing my hair at home was an ordeal for everybody—mainly Mother, Bessie Grey (Thurza's daughter and my playmate) and me.

Mother tried to make a game of it. She'd get everything ready: the coconut oil shampoo, the bowl on a chair with newspapers spread all around, two pitchers of water, plenty of towels. Then as she ducked my head into the bowl of warm water, she would recite:

Baptise Peter.
Baptise Paul.
Baptise little girl—
Head and all!

Bessie Grey poured the water to rinse the soap suds out of my hair. Mother brushed out the tangles. I cried the whole time. Soap got in my eyes. Water got in my ears and up my nose. Getting the tangles out pulled and hurt. (When I woke up with tangled hair in the mornings, Thurza used to tell me the witches had ridden me all night.)

So Mother began sending me to the barber shop to get my shampoos. First I went to Dad Wynn's, which was next to the Hille Hotel. He would lift me onto the black leather seat of his barber chair, get out his straight razor and pretend he was going to give me a shave.

When I protested, he replied in mock surprise, "No shave? O, I remember, it's a shampoo you want!" Then he'd lather my straight hair and pull it up into a peak, like a Kewpie doll.

"Now look," and he would turn the chair around so I could see myself in the long mirror.

Above the bottles of brilliantine, bay rum, orrisroot and witch hazel, above the combs in tall glass cylinders, the clippers and tickley brushes, a stranger stared back at me.

"Let's just leave it like that—you look pretty!" Dad Wynn would tease. "Go show the folks at the hotel how pretty you look." And he'd lift me out of the chair, tuck up the front of the cape so I wouldn't trip, and open the door for me. Trailing the barber cloth like a train, I, dutiful child, ran to the hotel lobby to be "mirated over" (one of Aunt Bet's expressions) and petted.

Back in the barber shop, Dad Wynn and I finished the shampoo with me leaning over the lavatory while he sprayed tepid water on my head from a hose attached to the faucet. A final combing, trimming of my bangs, dusting around my neck with Mavis powder ("I want you to smell like you've been to the barber shop") and I was ready to leave.

I could hear Dad Wynn shaking his barber cloth, giving it sharp little pops, as I walked toward the bank to show Daddy how I looked.

I don't know why I stopped going to Dad Wynn's barbershop and started letting Mr. Luther Moore shampoo my hair. Maybe Dad Wynn retired or died or moved away. I don't know. I continued to tolerate the teasing at Mr. Luther Moore's shop until "Miss Coral" Walker opened Thomasville's first beauty parlor. I was one of her early customers.

Miss Coral had her beauty parlor in her home, a squat yellow house with a porch around three sides and a huge pecan tree in the back yard. She had moved back to Thomasville after her husband died, bringing her daughter, who was in the eleventh grade, and her twelve-year-old son, Lyles Carter.

Lyles Carter

LYLES CARTER was the first boy I ever loved.

It was recess time, soon after school had started, and a cluster of us fifth grade girls were standing in the shade of an oak tree, watching the boys down on the football field. They were having a race, and a boy I had never seen before won easily. They ran again, sprinting toward the goal post at the opposite end of the field, and again he won. He was blond and slender, moved with an easy grace. Now I might describe him as lithe, but I didn't know that word then.

A few days later, he sent me a note written on tablet paper and folded into a tight triangle, the way notes were folded then. "If you like me write back," it said. I wrote back. All that year, the year he was in the sixth grade and I was in the fifth, we exchanged notes. Sometimes we'd slip them to each other as we passed in the hall. Sometimes we hid them behind a loose brick in the retaining wall at the edge of the campus. Often we employed the use of couriers.

I saved all those notes from Lyles Carter, stuffed them into an empty space above the door of my old playhouse under the chinaberry tree in our back yard.

Lyles Carter was always in trouble with the grammar school principal, Marion Pearce. She liked him, admired his quick mind and enjoyed his sense of humor, but she could not accept his non-conformist, often openly rebellious attitude toward her rules. Miss Pearce (there were rumors that she smoked) was a strict disciplinarian, and she whipped Lyles Carter nearly every day. Sometimes he was innocent of the offense for which he was punished.

There was, for instance, the day someone brought a frog into the fifth grade room during the noon recess. A few of us played with the frog (I did not believe that handling frogs caused warts), and then Ruth put it in Minnie Belle Wilson's desk. It hopped out.

I captured it and, to the amusement of the onlookers, put it in Miss Pearce's desk drawer. I don't think I meant to leave it there, but before I could retrieve it, the bell rang and Miss Pearce walked into the room. She opened her drawer to get her roll book, and out hopped the frog. She was not frightened, just enraged. I don't believe I ever saw her angrier.

She did not say a word. Her dark eyes scanned the classroom. Every pupil was busy studying—Ruth and I most studious of all!

She sent for Lyles Carter. As soon as he entered the room, she showered him with a torrent of accusations, giving him no opportunity to deny her charges.

I was about to admit my guilt when Lyles Carter looked at me and shook his head. So I sat still and watched as Miss Pearce took him into the dark office down the hall, listened to the licks as she hit him with her switch.

As soon as Miss Pearce returned to the room, I asked permission to go get a drink of water. I was not thirsty—I wanted to see Lyles Carter, wanted to let him know I thought he was wonderful. He was sitting in Miss Pearce's chair, whirling around in it. I waved at him, and he smiled at me, a smile of love and protection. We never mentioned the incident, not until we were grown.

I don't remember what summer it was that Lyles Carter shot his toe off. Maybe it wasn't summertime when the accident happened. Maybe it happened the fall after he won the tree sitting contest. Anyhow, he rested the barrel of his .22 rifle on his foot, and it discharged, completely severing the toe next to his big toe.

"It really didn't hurt much," he told me. "I'm just glad it wasn't my big toe! And now I really leave a peculiar track when I walk barefooted. Just call me Old Nine Toes." So a toe was gone and the corner of one of his front teeth was broken off, but I still thought he was perfect.

I heard that he drew obscene pictures on the blackboard. One recess I walked into the classroom and saw him at the board with laughing boys clustered around him. As soon as he saw me, he erased whatever he had drawn. When I returned, the board was covered with hearts enclosing our initials: KT and LCW. He left them there for everybody to see.

Teace told me he had carved a big heart with our initials in it up in the tip-top of the tall beech tree at the edge of Gunn's pasture. He never told me about it, and I never climbed up that high in the tree to see it for myself.

I did climb up into the pecan tree in his back yard the summer, about 1930, when Lyles Carter and Grey Beagle entered the Clarke County Tree-Sitting contest. Tree-sitting was a fad that Depression year, a diversion to take people's minds off hard times, I suppose.

There was a tree house in the big limbs of that pecan tree, a platform about six feet square with a roof and sides maybe two feet high. The structure had been up there among the leaves long before the tree-sitting craze swept the country. Lyles Carter and Grey took a notion it was just right for tree-sitting. They intended, they said, to be the champions of the county, to stay up in a tree longer than anybody else did.

Most folks thought the boys would come down after the first night, after a night of isolation, darkness and mosquitoes, but they didn't. They stayed up in that tree almost two weeks, and they did indeed become the Tree Sitting Champions of Clarke County.

Their mamas took turns fixing their meals, sending them up in the wooden box the boys lowered and hoisted by ropes. The mamas also sent up soap, buckets of hot water and towels every two or three days, but I'm not sure those supplies were used.

I climbed up to visit once or twice, taking with me copies of "The Christian Observer" which had a continued story I thought they would enjoy reading. Later I heard they didn't read anything up there in their sanctuary—they played poker!

As I recall, the rewards Lyles Carter and Grey received for their tree-sitting feat were getting their names in the paper (the news account was disappointingly brief) and three dozen popsicles. The greatest reward, some neighbors said, was Miss Coral's: Lyles Carter sojourn in the pecan tree was the longest period of time in his whole life that she knew where he was!

Daddy never liked Lyles Carter. I don't know why. He never said anything against him, never forbade me to see him, but his disapproval, though silent, was obvious.

Our telephone was on the wall in the dining room, and it seemed that Lyles Carter always called me at mealtime. Our conversations—at least my part—were brief and impersonal. I couldn't even say, "I'm glad you called," with Daddy listening.

Usually we met at Aunt Bet's house. Lyles Carter would walk over (I don't recall that he ever even owned a bicycle) after supper and I would be waiting for him there. In the long summer twilights we played croquet under Aunt Bet's pecan trees. We played card games (he always won) and a board game called Camelot (I always won). Sometimes Lyles Carter helped Aunt Bet work crossword puzzles and cryptoquotes. He would have loved playing Scrabble, but it hadn't been invented then. One winter Aunt Bet taught him to crochet, and they made a stocking-top rug.

Lyles Carter was a good cook, and he liked to try out new recipes in Aunt Bet's kitchen. His specialty was a concoction so rich that only he and I could eat it: begin by boiling a can of Eagle Brand sweetened condensed milk for two hours or more. Let it cool. Open can at both ends and push out the caramelized contents. Roll it in chopped pecans, slice and eat.

Lyles Carter gave me four gifts: a bookcase he made himself, a Richard Hudnut make-up set, an art deco desk lamp made of silver metal with a red arrow shooting through it, and a pair of wine and gold shoes.

The bookcase was made of a wooden crate painted bright blue. He brought it to me the summer I was twelve and was in bed with a heavy cast on my leg, the result of a knee injury. He came often to see me those long, hot afternoons.

The compact and lipstick were a Christmas gift when I was a senior in high school. Lyles Carter was working in Bedsole's during the holiday season (his mother had moved her beauty parlor from their home into quarters on the second floor of Bedsole's), learning, he said, that he did not want to be a salesman.

I walked into Bedsole's on Christmas Eve and, while I chatted with Miss Jodie, I saw Lyles Carter get the set out of a glass showcase and take it to the office in the rear of the store. There on the long counter where the dumbwaiter moved up and down between the first and second floors all day long, where the heavy roll of Bedsole's wrapping paper anchored one end, where Lucy Ora checked each sales slip, he wrapped the set clumsily in excessive layers of white tissue paper. Then he handed it to Teace (she also had a holiday season job at Bedsole's) who brought it to the front of the store and handed it to me. There was no card.

The lamp was a high school graduation gift and went off to college with me.

The shoes, sandals made of camel hide, came from North Africa when he was stationed there as a lieutenant with the Army Engineers, during World War II. He met—and married—Patsy, an English dancer, there in North Africa.

I wish that Daddy could have known that Lyles Carter married someone else, not me.

Miss Lillie

FROM THEIR TREE HOUSE, Lyles Carter and Grey Beagle could—if they wanted to—look across to Miss Lillie Harrison's home, could see the garden where Miss Lillie's husband, Henry (she called him Hendry) worked every day. It was the neatest, cleanest, most perfect garden in Thomasville. When he finished working every afternoon, Mr. Henry used to back out of the garden, raking as he went, so he would not mar the garden's perfection by leaving footprints in it.

Miss Lillie took in sewing. She had one of Thomasville's earliest industries, employing six or eight women to sew for her in her home. She had four sewing machines, the pedal kind, in the front room to the left of the hall, and three more machines against the wall down that long hall.

In the fall, when new school dresses were needed, all the machines whirred, just as they did in the spring when the demand for Easter dresses was great. Miss Lillie made my school dresses and my Easter dresses—Mother's sewing skills were limited to simple projects, such as covering porch pillows.

Miss Lillie did little sewing herself. Mainly she pinned the patterns to the cloth (she could line up a row of a dozen pins between her lips—said it was easier and quicker than using a pincushion—and still carry on a conversation) and did the cutting. She also supervised the stitching at each machine.

Miss Jodie, of course, helped Mother select the patterns, the materials and the trimmings for my dresses. I did not always like what she chose, but I was never consulted, and I never remember complaining—except about a stiff dotted-swiss Easter dress that scratched my neck and armpits and a navy blue sailor that looked like so many other sailor dresses I felt I was wearing a uniform.

My bedroom, the front room with the bay window, did not have a closet, so my dresses hung on hangers from a wire stretched along the wall behind the door. I took those two dresses off their hangers.

Miss Lillie fitted the dresses (sometimes it took three trips to her house before the fit satisfied her) and leveled the hems at the final fitting. She used to kneel on the bare floor for this ritual, but after she got older, added some pounds and her bones got stiff, "Hendry" built a small wooden platform for her customers to stand on while she pinned up their hems. I stumped my toes lots of times on that platform.

Mr. Henry seldom came into the front of the house, at least not in the daytime when the sewing was in progress. He used the door by the kitchen and stayed in the back rooms, out of respect for his wife's customers who might be trying on garments. He died not long after the couple celebrated their golden wedding anniversary.

Miss Lillie was well fixed, owned a home, a farm (she liked to refer to it as "the plantation") out from town, a car and her sewing business. She was lonesome though.

One afternoon a tall, gangling man with a peculiar accent got off the train and asked at the depot where Mrs. Lillian Harrison lived. About an hour later, the couple appeared at the Baptist pastorium to be married. The preacher performed the ceremony with his wife as the witness. The groom's name was Alfred Bathe, and he was from Minnesota, or some such far away place. He was considerably younger than Miss Lillie.

Word got out about Miss Lillie's marriage (Aunt Bet would say, "It was norated around") and there was some concern about her taking up with a strange man, a mail order husband. The preacher's wife was so upset she wanted him to go to the Harrison-Bathe house that night to make sure Miss Lillie was all right. He refused to go.

Miss Lillie and Mr. Alfred had a happy marriage. He never was as good a gardener as Mr. Henry had been, but it turned out that he was a fine house painter.

Expression

OCCASIONALLY LYLES CARTER AND I played the piano. When he was a senior in high school, he began taking piano lessons (he did not take from Cousin Golda) so he could learn to play "The Scarf Dance." He mastered that composition, could play it beautifully, but then he wanted to expand his repertoire. We would get old copies of "The Etude" out of Tabb's piano bench and play the simple duets printed in them. Usually, after only a few measures, Tabb came in and took over my part.

I just never could play the piano. But if my musical career was a fiasco, I compensated by excelling in what was called "expression." I took expression, as did most of my friends, from Mrs. McIntosh, an imposing woman with red curly hair, who came to Thomasville on the train from Catherine to give lessons.

Actually, Tabb was my first expression teacher. Long before I was old enough to go to school, she taught me little speeches so she could show me off at the Post Office. My stage was the long wooden table, flanked by tall pigeonholes, where mail sacks were emptied and where, during the summer, big watermelons brought in by rural mail carriers, or bought off a farm wagon for fifteen cents, were cut daily.

Lifted up to the table by one of the clerks, Clio McCrory or Jimmy Megginson, or perhaps by Tabb, I would recite:

> Here I stand
> Black and dirty.
> If you don't come kiss me,
> I'll run like a turkey!

or

> I'm a cute little girl

With a cute little figger.
Stand back, boys,
'Til I get a little bigger.

Then I would turn and jump into someone's waiting arms. The applause and the laughter pleased me, as did the slice of watermelon or the lemon drop or the "wrist watch" postmark that was my reward.

The speeches Mrs. McIntosh taught me were of somewhat higher poetic quality, and they were much longer. Some dealt with dolls, broken and lost, one told reassuringly of the gentleness of the dark, and one, which Mother disliked, was an account of a family who spent a miserable Christmas because the mother was so busy taking cheer to orphans and prisoners that she neglected her own loved ones.

We didn't have much of a Christmas,
My papa and brother and me,
'Cause Mama had gone to the orphanage
To trim up the poor orphans' tree.

the poem began, and it got worse as it went along through many verses.

Few of my recitations were from the classics, but I did not care. They were words, not musical notes. I understood words, was comfortable with them. I memorized easily, and I looked forward eagerly to my weekly expression lessons.

However, Mrs. McIntosh and I did not always work in harmony. She believed in motions, natural and graceful motions. My motions were neither natural nor graceful.

"Move naturally. Lift your right arm gracefully on that line," she would instruct. "Gracefully! Let's try it again." Her interruptions annoyed me, and, under my breath, I called her "Old Lady McIntosh." She couldn't have been more than thirty-five.

When she began to prepare us for our expression recital, Mrs. McIntosh told us, "Remember that the people in the audience have come to hear what you have to say. So hold your head up, look at them and speak out! Speak out!"

It was at one of her expression recitals that I had my first encounter with a peeping Tom. The recital was held in the school auditorium, a brick building that sat in a grove of oak trees. The auditorium was where students had weekly chapel services, marching over in orderly fashion from the two-story frame schoolhouse about fifty feet away. Graduations, public speakings, plays, operettas, piano recitals (not Cousin Golda's), fiddler's conventions and such were also held in that building. The PTA had its touring art exhibits there. I guess it could have been called the cultural center of Thomasville.

Sometimes after I had been taken to an art exhibit or a concert or a lecture at the auditorium, I would complain that I had gotten nothing out of the event.

Mother's response was always,

Diving and finding
No pearls in the sea,
Blame not the ocean:
The fault is with thee.

I heard that bit of verse mighty often during my growing-up years.

The bricks at the rear of the auditorium, on the side nearest the schoolhouse, had a grey sheen of chalk dust absorbed from the beating of hundreds of blackboard erasers on their rough surfaces. To be given permission to go dust the erasers was a coveted privilege.

The inside of the auditorium, its rows of wooden folding seats scarred by the carved initials of generations of students, was ugly, but Mrs. McIntosh did what she could to make it attractive by putting tall wicker baskets of Dorothy Perkins roses on each side of the stage and using colored bulbs in the footlights.

The night of the peeping Tom episode we girls were waiting in the dressing room on the left of the stage for our turns to say our recitations. Mrs. McIntosh had the program with our order of appearances tacked on the wall. She sat in the audience on the front row so she could prompt us if we hesitated or forgot.

Just before time for the program to start, I was about to walk over to take another look at myself in the mirror nailed to the door (I was pleased with my pale blue accordion-pleated dress) when one of the older girls pulled me aside and whispered, "Don't walk over there. Somebody is under the floor trying to look up our dresses."

I tiptoed close to the spot where she pointed, and, surely enough, an eye was staring up from a knothole in the floor.

I never did tell Mother about that episode, didn't want to embarrass her. Later (three years? four?) I never told her that I knew where babies came from. I agonized for months over how to tell her that I knew, but I lacked the courage to do it. We never discussed money or sex in our family.

Illnesses

I MISSED ONE of Mrs. McIntosh's recitals, came down with some childhood illness the very day of the event. I don't recall what the ailment was. I know it wasn't the measles because I waited until I was in high school to have that disfiguring disease—and Mother let Elo Jackson, whom I liked very much at the time, come in to see me when I was broken out solid in the red rash and had not brushed my hair in two days. Elo laughed.

Family members tell me I was a sickly baby and a puny child.

One of my early memories is of being wrapped in a blanket and taken from my bed in the Selma Baptist Hospital across a field to the river bank to watch a steamboat go by. It was the first steamboat I had ever seen and was probably one of the last to ply the Alabama River.

I was a few years older, probably about seven or eight years old, when I had a prolonged stay in the Selma hospital. After I had recovered sufficiently, I came home on the train. As the train stopped at the Thomasville depot, I looked out the window and was pleased to see a group of my friends waiting beside the track—Evelyn, Teace, Rosamond, Billy, Robert and others.

I came slowly, as befitted a semi-invalid, down the steps of the train, expecting to hear a chorus of "We're glad you're home! Are you feeling better? We missed you!"

What I heard was one voice saying in disgust, "She ain't baldheaded!"

Word had gotten around that I had had such high fever the doctors shaved my head. My friends had come to see the hairless freak, not to welcome me home. It was a severe shock to my ego.

I nearly lost my hair—and my life—the summer when I was

four and had diphtheria. I remember two things about that illness:

My doctor brother Wood (Wood pitched a double-header, no-hit baseball game when he played for a semi-pro team in Bessemer, an exploit that got him in Ripley's "Believe It Or Not") came from Birmingham and gave me a shot with the biggest needle I ever saw.

My brother Wilson brought me a small turtle, one he picked up beside the road. He put the turtle in a blue enamel pan with water and rocks in it, and he set the pan on the floor where I could see it by peeping over the edge of the bed. Watching that turtle marked my first interest in anything (not even Tabb's shadow pictures of barking dogs and flying birds or Mother's stories or Daddy's harmonica playing or Thurza's promise of homemade peppermint ice cream had made me smile) after a string of listless days. I don't know whether it was the shot or the turtle that cured me.

There were other illnesses, none so serious as the diphtheria, and I claimed the distinction of being the only person in Thomasville who had had two separate surgeries, some six years apart, for the removal of tonsils and adenoids. Mine grew back.

Mother kept a supply of medicines for minor upsets—syrup of figs, Fletcher's Castoria, S.S.S. Tonic, Wampole's Cod Liver Oil—lined up against the back of her wash stand where they left sticky stains on the embroidered runner.

Doses from those bottles were administered when I was well and active, to ward off illness, I suppose. The really awful medicines were given when I was sick abed, too weak and feverish to escape.

If the doctor came, as he usually did, he left what were called "little powders," premeasured doses of white powdered curatives, which he compounded and brought in his black satchel. Each dose was wrapped in white paper, like a chewing gum wrapper, and it was either to be thumped to the back of the tongue and washed down with big swallows of water, or dissolved in water in a big spoon and gulped down. Either way was bad.

Mother would take my temperature, putting the thermometer

in my armpit (I was in school before she deemed it safe for me to hold the thermometer in my mouth), to determine when I needed to take another "little powder."

Worse than the powders were the coco quinine and the castor oil I sometimes had to swallow. Mother would stand patiently beside my bed holding a spoonful of that horrible coco quinine and urging me to open my mouth.

"If you don't take this soon, my arm is going to get paralyzed, frozen in this position," she would say. Her words were not persuasive until she changed her tone of voice and said, "Kathryn, open your mouth." Then I opened, and she thrust the potion-filled spoon into my mouth. Horrible!

Even castor oil was not as foul-tasting as coco quinine. Maybe I felt more kindly toward castor oil because I had to take it less often.

"We're going to give you something to make you well," Mother would say pleasantly in a tone of voice used only when she was referring to castor oil.

She and Thurza used to try to administer the dose. "Just hold your nose and shut your eyes and swallow quick," Mother would say. "I've got something good to take the taste out," she promised. I was unpersuaded. It was a miserable time for us all.

So Mother began letting Mr. Theodore Megginson fix my dose of castor oil at Peoples Drug Store. I'd hear her telephone the order, and in a little while I'd hear Junior Stutts come whistling up the hill. Junior Stutts made deliveries for Peoples Drug Store on foot, and he whistled every step he took.

Mother would meet him at the door and take the Coca-Cola tray with the glass of castor oil, orange juice and carbonated water, all mixed together.

"Mr. Theodore say stir it a few times," Junior reminded Mother.

I tried to drink it all down in big gulps while it was still fizzing, but nothing disguised the castor oil smell and taste. Maybe it did make me well.

I'm not sure which of the Thomasville doctors prescribed those physics for me. Our town always had good—if somewhat eccentric—country doctors, family practitioners who made house calls whenever and wherever they were needed.

One of our best known doctors was Dr. A. L. White who delivered more babies than any doctor in the county, and who could spit farther than any tobacco-chewer along the whole Southern Railway System.

Dr. White had an office next door to Peoples Drug Store, but he didn't stay in it very much. If he wasn't out seeing about his patients, he was, weather permitting, sitting in a wicker rocking chair on the sidewalk in front of his office. He would rock slowly and read aloud from The Clarke County Democrat or The Christian Advocate, or a medical journal, droning along for an hour or more, through the lists of appointments of preachers in the Alabama-West Florida Conference or the notices of tax sales, or new methods of treating hook worm.

He always had an audience for his reading: overalled loafers sat along the edge of the high sidewalk, or squatted with their backs against his office wall. His listeners were careful to leave an ample opening between Doctor White and the street, knowing from experience that he would often stop in mid-sentence to spit, without warning, an amber arc of tobacco juice in that direction.

Dr. White did a lot of his diagnosing and some of his examinations out on the sidewalk. If a patient interrupted his reading, Dr. White would listen to the symptoms and then order, "Stick out your tongue."

While Dr. White examined the outstretched tongue, so did all the idlers. They clustered around the rocking chair, vying for the best view, somewhat like a team of specialists called in for consultation. However, they made no comments about diagnosis or treatment; Dr. White did not take kindly to unsolicited advice.

Dr. White had been known to lance abseses, sharpening his knife on the sole of his high top shoes, right there on the sidewalk. He did take his patients into the privacy of his cluttered office for more personal examinations.

That office was a storehouse for his medical journals (he kept abreast of modern medical practices) and a pantry for his bottles of pharmacopoeia. He mixed and dispensed his own medications, used to laugh and say his diagnosis often depended on what curative drugs he had on hand.

He used to tell about one of his patients for whom he prescribed a powerfully potent medicine in powder form.

"You don't want to take too much of this," Dr. White told his patient. "Take just as much as you can pile up on a dime."

A few days later when he went to see if the fellow's health had improved, Dr. White was greeted with, "Doctor, that medicine you gave me to take like to have killed me!"

"Did you take it the way I told you to, only as much as you could pile up on a dime?"

"Sure did. But nobody had a dime, so I used two nickels."

Dr. White liked to tell that tale.

He had a telephone in his office, but he seldom used it. The telephone operator could ring and ring and ring his number (from her upstairs window in the telephone office she could see him sitting out on the sidewalk), but he would not answer. He claimed access to a telephone made it too easy for people to be sick.

"A fellow will feel bad, maybe have a little pain somewhere, and, just because a telephone is handy, he'll call a doctor. If somebody really needs me, he'll come to my office or he'll send me word to come see him.

"And besides, I can't diagnose ailments over the telephone! I've got to look at folks' tongues and take their pulse and see the whites of their eyes."

So when folks wanted to get in touch with Dr. White, they called Peoples' Drug Store and a soda jerker would go deliver the message.

The only time anybody could remember Dr. White talking over the telephone was once when he called Birmingham to get rabies serum for a child who had been bitten by a mad dog.

Dr. White was a bit peculiar, but his patients loved him, loved him with a love reserved for someone who has shared the wonder of life's beginning and the bewilderment of its ending.

I really don't believe it was Dr. White who prescribed coco quinine or castor oil for me. But I know it was Mrs. Johnson (most people called her Mama Sue) who made me eat gruel when I was sick. Mrs. Johnson was our neighbor down on the corner, across from the Methodist Church. She lived in a cream colored house with steep, narrow concrete steps leading up to her vine-shaded porch. Her front gate had a heavy weight on it to make it close tight.

By that gate was a rose bush that bore small red blossoms most of the year. I used to pick a rose from that bush and take it to Daddy when I walked past on my way to see him at the bank. He wore the blossom on his lapel.

Mrs Johnson was small and thin, and she pulled her scrawny gray hair into a tight knot on top of her head, so tight that it almost smoothed out the wrinkles in her face. She wore cotton print dresses down to her shoe tops, and she put on a fresh apron every day. I thought she had snuff in her apron pocket, but I never was sure.

She kept house for her daughter, Susie, who stopped working as a stenographer (all the keys on her typewriter were covered with black rubber caps) after her hip was injured in an automobile accident, and for her son, Albert, who was a lawyer and owned about as much land as Mr. Cogle did.

When I missed two or three days coming by her house to pick a rose for Daddy, or to swing in the double swing on her porch, or to wind up her Victrola and play "Listen To The Mocking Bird," she would know I was sick. She would telephone Mother, "Helen, I am bringing Kathryn some gruel."

Mother would say to me, "That was Mrs. Johnson." I knew the rest.

She not only brought the gruel, a thin, watery, warm, tasteless mixture of corn meal and water, she sat beside my bed until I ate every spoonful in the bowl.

"Gruel is strengthening, will make you better," she would say in her nasal voice, a voice as thin as the gruel. "I'll make gingerbread men for you when you're well. Eat your gruel. All of it." I ate. I had no choice.

Mrs. Johnson did make good gingerbread men, big ones with lots of raisin buttons on their coats.

However, it was not her gingerbread men or her roses or even the swing on her porch that lured me to her house: it was Susie.

Town Characters

SUSIE SUBSCRIBED to every movie magazine she knew about. Copies of *Photoplay, Silver Screen, Motion Picture World*, were stacked along the wall in her bedroom, right beside her vanity table with its triple mirrors. Susie kept her Dr. Blosser's cigarettes in the left hand top drawer of that vanity. She was the first woman I ever saw smoke, and, even though she explained that the medicated cigarettes were prescribed by a doctor to relieve her sinus condition, I considered her sophisticated and even a little wicked.

Later, when I was in junior high school and wrote movie reviews for my Cousin Earl's newspaper in exchange for a pass to the picture show, I found Susie's movie magazines invaluable reference sources.

Susie had remarkable pets. She had canaries in cages in nearly every room, and she had trained them to sing in unison whenever she played the piano. Susie wasn't able to type after her automobile accident, but she could play ragtime loud enough to be heard all over our end of town. She did not play ragtime often because, she explained, it drowned out the singing of her birds and hurt their feelings.

Occasionally her dog, a Doberman named Reddy Boy, would add his bass voice to the concert. Susie said Reddy Boy could talk. He did use to order his meaty bones from Jeff Larrimore's market. Susie would get the telephone operator (Central, we called her) to ring the market, and Reddy Boy would bark his order into the telephone mouthpiece. In a few minutes, his bone would be delivered, and Reddy Boy, at Susie's prompting, would bark what sounded like "Thank you."

It was Reddy Boy who saved the Johnsons' house from burning up. Susie saw the whole episode and told everybody about it. She said an electric extension cord near her bedroom suddenly burst into flame. She, being crippled from her accident, couldn't hobble to the kitchen to get water to put out the fire, and Little Mama Sue was too deaf to hear the commotion. Albert was at his law office.

Reddy Boy immediately comprehended the seriousness of the situation. He, Susie said, heisted his hind leg, aimed and doused the flames before they spread. She thought Reddy Boy deserved a medal for his quick-thinking heroism.

Susie also had cats, six of them as I recall. They and Reddy Boy got along fine together. The cats slept in doll beds on the back screened porch. Each cat had its own bed with its name on it, and at naptime and bedtime each cat slept in its assigned bed. The beds even had sheets and little pillows, though I don't believe they were monogrammed.

There was nothing unusual about the goldfish Susie had, but her four tame turkeys were amazing; they could tap dance. Susie said they could. They learned to dance, Susie said, by watching Anita Fleming, who lived in Mobile and used to come visit her Aunt Vera Moore (Mr. Luther Moore's wife) every summer. The Moores' back yard and the Johnsons' back yard were separated by a high board fence.

Anita, who was a year or so younger than I was, took tap dancing in Mobile. Nobody in Thomasville took tap dancing—or any other kind. Anita would bring her tap shoes and her costumes (pink and yellow short skirts made of layers of ruffled tarlatan with spangled tops) when she came for her summer visits, and she would put on shows for the neighborhood children in the Moores' back yard. We envied her costumes almost as much as we did her dancing ability. The only costumes we had were made out of crepe paper for school plays, and they didn't last much longer than did the outfits we fashioned of big cowcumber leaves when we played in Hill's pasture.

Well, Susie said her turkeys peeped through the cracks in the fence every time Anita gave one of her performances, and they learned to tap dance. Every time they heard lively music, they would start dancing like Anita, Susie said. Some Sunday mornings, while the Methodist congregation across the street sang rousing hymns, those turkeys danced all around the back yard. Susie talked once about getting some little tap shoes made for her turkeys, but I don't think she ever did.

It was at the Johnson home that I heard my first radio. It was a crystal set. I couldn't have been more than three years old, but I remember Susie put earphones on me and moved a wire around until I assured her that I "heard something." I think all I heard was static.

I suppose swallowing Mrs. Johnson's gruel was a small price to pay for all the entertainment and close friendship that family gave me.

For as long as I lived at home, I took Mrs. Johnson a May basket on May Day each year, a basket I made of construction paper and filled with flowers from our yard. I would go early in the morning, tie the basket to her door knob with a pastel ribbon, knock loudly and then run so she—or whoever came to the door—could not see who had left the basket. All during my childhood, Mother helped me fix May baskets to deliver secretly to neighbors, but Mrs. Johnson was the only one for whom I continued the custom.

When I laughed at Susie's peculiarities, or somebody else's, Daddy would say, "Don't forget about your Uncle Wilmer. He does some strange things, too, and he's your uncle. Maybe we are all 'teched in the haid.' Makes us interesting."

Uncle Wilmer, Daddy's brother who lived in Grove Hill, did indeed do some strange things. He was a quiet man, smaller than his eight brothers, and he earned a living by dealing in oil leases. I never was sure exactly what that meant. So far as I know, nobody ever struck oil in Clarke County.

Somewhere Uncle Wilmer had learned to read lips. He used to stand on the street and watch people's conversations, recording what they said in a little notebook he carried with him. The importance of the conversations seemed not to matter: he recorded discussions of pending court cases and law suits right along with comments on the weather and baseball games.

Some people said Uncle Wilmer used to stand in an upstairs window at Peerless Drug Company (his brother, Bertie, owned the drug store) with a pair of field glasses and watch conversations all up and down both sides of the street. Being on a corner with windows facing two streets, the drug store was a fine vantage point for Uncle Wilmer's avocation.

His favorite spot for collecting conversations, however, was a local restaurant where men gathered for coffee every morning. He recorded pages and pages of talk there—until the men caught on to what he was doing.

After they caught on, encroaching on their conversations became more difficult for Uncle Wilmer. As soon as he would enter the cafe, everybody would stop talking. There was absolute silence except for the noise from the kitchen and an occasional laugh from a table of men.

The men wrote notes to each other, scribbling them on paper napkins or the backs of envelopes and passing them around the table. Then, when they finished their coffee and got ready to leave, the men tore their notes into little pieces and left them on the table.

Uncle Wilmer, they say, would gather up the scraps of paper and put them in his coat pocket. Later he would spend hours piecing them together, like a jigsaw puzzle.

When he died, they say Uncle Wilmer left a trunkful of those scraps of paper and of small notebooks, a serigamy of them, filled with conversations. I never saw them, just heard about them. I don't know whether Daddy ever saw them or not. But I haven't forgotten my Uncle Wilmer. Nor have I forgotten Daddy's observation that "maybe we're all a little 'teched in the haid.'"

Trains, Circuses, and Tent Shows

IT MUST HAVE BEEN AUNT BET who first got me interested in trains, who made me wonder what the boxcars held, where they were going, where they had been. I think Aunt Bet would have liked to be a hobo.

She and I never tired of watching the trains. Their whistles called me from play, and I would lean against the front porch bannisters, counting the freight cars that rolled past. That's how I learned to count. The double-headers (two steam engines) pulled strings of cars so long I'd have to count to one hundred and start over again.

Usually the engines stopped at the big wooden water tank that stood on creosoted pilings to "get a drink," Daddy used to say. I'd watch as the crewmen pulled down the metal spout to fill the train's boiler, and I'd listen for the creak as they released the chain and the spout swung up against the tank again.

In the summertime it was always cool and damp under the water tank, and in the winter we measured the severity of the cold by the size of the icicles that hung from its sides.

Our lives were in large measure regulated by trains. Aunt Bet and Tabb were always at the Post Office to put up the mail, no matter how far behind schedule the passenger train with its mail car was. Sometimes they left their supper half-eaten to hurry to the Post Office and put up the mail. As a child, the blowing of the 7:40 train whistle at night was the signal for my bedtime. Wakefulness was reported by, "I didn't go to sleep until after the midnight freight ran."

Meeting the train was something of a social event in Thomasville, just as it was in other small towns. The conductor brought news from up and down the line: a good rain at Arlington, a new Baptist preacher at Marion Junction, Dr. Fudge ill at Lamison, fish biting at McIntosh, another baseball game won by the team at Jackson, all sorts of news.

The one person who met every train (maybe he missed the midnight freight—I don't know) was Mallie Jackson. Mallie thought he was in charge of the railroad, and I guess he was in a way. Mallie was for years the official-unofficial guard at the railroad crossing in Thomasville. The crossing had no warning lights, no gates, so Mallie positioned himself beside the tracks and waved traffic to a halt when a train was approaching.

Mallie's left arm was withered and crooked and his left leg was shorter than his right, giving him a hopping gait as he hurried about his railroad duties. He lived a mile or so down the railroad from town, but he spent every day guarding the Thomasville crossing.

The railroad men humored him by giving him a red bandana and a railroad cap to wear, replacing them as needed. The cap, which Mallie considered his badge of authority, had to be lapped over and pinned to fit his small head. Nobody ever saw Mallie without his railroad cap on. Some folks said he slept in it.

Right often men in Luther Moore's barber shop or Eddie's Cafe or the freight office, places where Mallie hung out between trains, would threaten to steal his cap or would pretend that the railroad president had sent word to the sheriff to put Mallie in jail for trespassing.

Such teasings sent Mallie into frenzies of anger, just as his tormenters knew they would. They howled with laughter as Mallie, his face and neck as red as his bandana, described in his high-pitched voice how he was going to carve up his adversaries and dispose of their body parts. Only the fortuitous arrival of a train or the repeated assurances that they meant no harm saved the men from Mallie's threats.

It was those same seemingly heartless men who saw that Mallie had a hot bath in the back of the barber shop occasionally, who treated him to meals at The City Cafe or Eddie's Place, and who outfitted him with new shoes and clothes when he needed them. Best of all, they always stopped at the railroad crossing when Mallie waved them down, even if no train was in sound or sight. There never was a wreck at that crossing, not as long as Mallie guarded it.

About once a year when I watched the trains I saw brightly painted circus cars go past, big circuses on their way to Birmingham or Montgomery or Mobile. If the engine stopped for water, I'd have time to run down the hill for a closer look at the cars with their cages of lions, tigers, monkeys and zebras. Once a laughing hyena shrieked at me. No big circus ever came to Thomasville, of course. Few of any size did.

Once when I was a little girl, Mother and Tabb took me to Grove Hill to see a one-ring circus. Grove Hill, twelve miles away, was the county seat, so I suppose that town attracted more cultural events, such as circuses, than Thomasville did.

We three had seats right at ringside, on the second row. I could see everything. The final act of the show was to demonstrate the strength of the elephant (there was only one elephant in the circus, only one of anything) by letting him pull up a big metal stake in the center of the ring. The trainer put a heavy chain around the elephant's neck and tied the end to the stake, wrapping it around several times. Then he signaled the elephant to pull. He pulled. Nothing happened. He pulled again. Still nothing happened. The trainer shouted, prodded the animal with a spiked pole. The elephant roared his displeasure. People around us began to stir uneasily. The trainer shouted and prodded again.

The elephant responded with rage. He shifted his position in the ring until his backside was right at Mother, Tabb and me. I had never been so close to an elephant before. He strained at the chain, stomping his front feet and bellowing in frustration and anger. His rear end was almost in our laps, and if the stake had pulled loose, it would have been. The trainer ran from one side of his charge to the other, pushing and shoving and screaming commands in a futile effort to regain control. People began running from the tent. Mr. Clifton Gilmore, who had been sitting near us, snatched me up and shouted to Mother and Tabb, "Run! Run!" They did.

When we were safely outside, someone asked, "Mrs. Tucker, weren't you scared to death?"

"Well, no," Mother replied. "I was too occupied with wondering how our remains would be disposed of. I knew Mr. Tucker would never claim our bodies if we met our deaths by being sat on by an elephant!"

The next elephants I saw were at a safe distance. One morning, long before daylight, Daddy came into my room and shook me gently.

"Get up and dress—we're going to Montgomery to the circus!" he said. "Heddie has breakfast ready for us."

"Today? Now? But don't I have to go to school? It's a school day," I replied. I was in the fifth grade. I was already out of bed looking for clothes to wear.

"No school for you today. You and I are going to the circus," Daddy reassured me. "Hurry!" I hurried.

And so we set out for Montgomery, one hundred and twenty miles away, Daddy and I and his driver. Daddy had lost the sight in one eye and did not feel confident driving, so he hired drivers as he needed them. I don't remember how long the trip took. I don't remember what—or if—we ate. I don't remember what the weather was. I do remember the swirling lights, the rousing band music, the noisy excitement, the melding of odors, the difficulty in choosing which ring to watch.

I laughed at Emmett Kelly, sad-faced in his ragged clown costume. I saw Lillian Leitzel high on the flying trapeze. I saw Professor Zacchini shot from a cannon. I saw the Wallenda family on the high wire. I saw the Greatest Show On Earth, Ringling Brothers, Barnum and Bailey, and I saw it all with my daddy.

If the circuses did not come to Thomasville, the Cooke Players did. The week that traveling troupe came to town was the most exciting week of the year. Until they arrived, the only live theatre we saw was the play put on by the senior class each spring and the Masonic Lodge's annual black face minstrel. Their tour schedule brought them to Thomasville in the fall, and they put up their tent on the lot behind Dozier Hardware Company, across from the Baptist Church.

Since Daddy was a member of the Town Council, our whole family got free passes to the shows for all six nights. After supper, when I could not wait another minute to go to the tent, Mother would brush my hair and give me a fresh handkerchief with a dime tied in one corner. The dime was to buy candy ("A prize in each and every box!") between acts.

When I crossed the railroad tracks and walked up the hill to the tent, Mr. Cooke, in a little booth where he sold tickets outside the tent would greet me with "Go right in, young lady, and get a good seat." He made me feel very grown-up.

Once inside, I'd walk up the grassy aisle and choose my seat, a hard folding chair right up front. I was always early enough to get a choice seat. Then, while I waited for other people to arrive and for the play to begin, I would finger my dime and listen to Mrs. Cooke play ragtime on a tinny piano.

At curtain time, when the tent was nearly full and when he was sure he would sell no more tickets, Mr. Cooke would come inside to welcome the audience, to say how delighted they all were to be back in our "splendid little town" again.

Then he'd read the advertisements from "the progressive business firms who invite your patronage." Even the feed store's ad for laying mash sounded exciting the way Mr. Cooke read it. I knew the curtain was about to be pulled when he finished the ads, announced the name of the play (my favorite was "Over The Hill To the Poor House," a teary melodrama usually performed on Saturday night) and said with a dramatic flourish,

"If the baby cries, please take him out!"
He said that before every play, every year. We still say it in our family.

Mr. Cooke appeared again between acts to promote the sale of candy, bright boxes of gooey kisses, each stuck to its paper wrapper, with the promise of exciting prizes. My prize was nearly always a brass ring with a glass stone or a tin whistle or a tiny plaster animal. Once I found in my box a "valuable coupon good for fine merchandise displayed on the stage." My coupon won me a gaudy blanket, an Indian blanket, Mr. Cooke said. It was the only prize I ever won.

While I ate my candy and waited for the show to continue, I worried about the fate of the gentle old couple and their beautiful daughter, Nell, worried lest they fail to escape from the clutches of the evil villain with the mustache (I never bought my between-acts candy from him—I recognized him even without his mustache) who threatened to foreclose the mortgage or to force Nell to become his wife.

I sat tense and wide-eyed until the handsome hero arrived with cash to pay off the mortgage just before the third act curtain. I was happier than anybody when the hero shouted, "Unhand her, you villain!" and kissed Nell.

After the curtain closed and the applause ended, I would meet my family at the ticket booth. They would walk ahead, laughing about the play and commenting on friends they had seen there. I would lag behind, holding on to the magic I had been a part of.

"Come on!" Mother would call. "You'll never get home at that rate. And it's already long past your bedtime!"

Mother never knew that I was Nell, waiting to be rescued by her lover, not a little girl being hurried home to bed.

Christmas

DADDY HAD A SAYING that he used when I would say, as all children do, "I want. . . ."

"You're big enough for your wants not to hurt you," Daddy would reply.

Maybe I wasn't quite big enough for my wants not to hurt me the Christmas I wanted a red scooter. I was five or six years old. Even before the Lions Club put up the Community Christmas tree in Clay Park, I knew that the only thing I really wanted Santa Claus to bring me was a scooter.

My friend, Little Edith, (her mother was named Edith so she, even after she was grown, was called Little Edith) had a scooter, but she was very particular about who rode it and where and for how long.

"You can ride my scooter down the front and around the side of the church two times," she would say. The Methodist Church had a paved sidewalk across the front and down one side, about the only sidewalk in Thomasville where we could ride scooters and skate. "Just two times. And don't get any scratches on my scooter!"

It wasn't much fun to ride Little Edith's scooter. I wanted one of my own, wanted Santa Claus to bring me one. I did not tell anybody what I wanted for Christmas; I believed with the faith of a child that Santa Claus knew about such things. On those days before Christmas, I did not ask Little Edith to let me ride her scooter. I could wait, wait until Santa Claus brought me a scooter of my very own.

Christmas morning I waked early, afraid to open my eyes for fear Santa Claus had not come. I peeped from under the covers and saw my stocking silhouetted against the fire, not hanging limp and empty the way I had nailed it up the night before, but lumpy and bulgy with surprises from Santa.

A jumping jack peeped out of the top.

I sat on the rug in front of the fire, exploring the contents of that plain cotton stocking: an orange, a deck of Old Maid cards, a satsuma, raisins with seeds in them, stick candy, other small gifts and, down in the toe, a dime wrapped in tissue paper. That dime in tissue paper was a tradition in Mother's family for as far back as anybody could recall.

The stocking was fine, but I was eager to go into the living room where the Christmas tree was, where I knew my scooter was waiting. Finally Daddy said, "I believe it is warm enough in the living room now," and he opened the door.

He had lighted the candles on the cedar branches of the tree, and by the candle light I saw a new doll, a big ball, books—but no scooter. I tried to be happy with my presents, tried to hide my disappointment, but I could not understand why Santa had not brought my scooter.

Later, after breakfast, I heard Daddy say to Mother, "There's not one in town." They stopped talking when they saw me listening. Still later, I walked into the dining room in time to hear Daddy say to the telephone operator, "I want long distance. Selma." Mother hurried me out of the room, but I heard him saying, "Of course I know it's Christmas Day! That's why I'm calling!" I didn't hear what else he said.

Late that afternoon, Daddy said to me, "Let's walk down and see the train come in." Mother bundled me up, and Daddy and I walked to the depot in the chilly December dusk. The lights were on in the depot, but all the stores were dark. We waited, warming by the stove, until we heard the train blow for first crossing, and then we moved out to stand beside the tracks. Daddy held my hand. When the train stopped, we were standing beside the baggage car. The door opened, and there in the lighted car was the baggageman holding a red scooter.

"Is your name Kathryn?" he asked me.

"Yes, sir."

"Well, then this scooter is for you. Santa Claus made a mistake and put it out at the wrong house, up around Arlington, I believe. He asked me to bring it to you."

He handed it down to me, the most beautiful scooter I'd ever seen! It wasn't until years later that I learned how my scooter got to me. Daddy, sensing my disappointment over Santa's failure, called his banker friend, Mr. Henry Plant, in Selma on Christmas morning and asked him to use his influence to get a scooter (preferably red) put aboard the southbound train for Thomasville that afternoon. Mr. Plant protested against such a request on Christmas Day, but my Daddy could be very persuasive when the occasion required.

The Christmases at our house were always touched by excitement and wonder. The celebration began in early November, and began so simply and quietly that I was hardly aware of its advent. On a November morning the train from Mobile would bring a rather small, brown, oblong package addressed to Mother.

"My narcissus bulbs have come from Van Antwerp's," Mother would say, lifting the tubers from their wrappings. "I do hope they will bloom in time for Christmas." They always did. First the narcissus bowls, the small containers in which the bulbs were planted each year, had to be found. Mother never joined in the actual search for the bowls, though she did provide Thurza and me, the usual searchers, with clues as to where they might be hiding. I had the feeling that failure to locate the containers would jeopardize the arrival of Christmas, so I searched with great diligence.

Sometimes the bowls were pushed far back behind things on top of the bookshelves on the back porch where a thirty-year collection of "Tarbell's Teacher's Guide to The International Sunday School Lessons" shared shelf space with a complete set of Zane Grey's western novels and a scattering of Tom Swift's adventures. Some years they were hidden beneath Grandmother's turkey platter in the bottom of the sideboard. Most often they were found among the clutter in the Far Room.

The bowl I remember best was round and green and had three stubby legs. It was chipped, a disfigurement suffered when a broken fishing rod fell on it during their joint occupancy of The Far Room.

Once the bowls were found, they were washed, filled with pebbles (Where did Mother get them? Were they, too, sent by Van Antwerp's?), and Mother set the bulbs gently in place.

"Must not crowd them. Must give them room to grow." she would say. I suppose she was talking to me. Then water, freshly drawn from the well, was poured to the proper depth over the pebbles and around the bulbs. Thurza, while the planting was going on, would clear space on closet shelves to hold the bowls with their pebbles, water and bulbs.

Occasionally, in the following weeks, Mother would shine a flashlight on the dark shelves to assure herself that the bulbs were growing and to add water as needed. The rest of the family forgot about the bulbs. The busy excitement of preparing for The Day crowded out all thoughts of brown tubers with their unlikely promise of fragrant beauty.

At night, sitting around the fire and talking, the family picked out pecans and cut up candied fruit to go into the rich cakes Aunt Bet and Mother, with Thurza's help, would make. I was rewarded with slivers of sugary pineapple and slices of cherries if I helped pick out nuts instead of scraping the poker against the back of the fireplace to release fluttering clusters of soot.

If I persisted in scraping the soot and poking the fire, Aunt Bet was likely to say, "You know what happens to children who play in the fire." I knew. Thurza had told me. So, not wanting to run the risk of wetting my bed, I would hang up the poker and help with the pecans.

Bottles of scuppernong and blackberry wine, made for the purpose, would be brought out to use for soaking the raisins and currants that went into the cakes. Later, when the cakes were taken out of the oven after their long, slow baking, some of that wine was poured over them before they were wrapped in white cloths and stored in metal boxes to ripen for Christmas.

The homemade wine also flavored the ambrosia that was our traditional Christmas dinner dessert. Thurza grated the fresh coconut that went into the ambrosia. The oranges were peeled and cut up as we sat around the fire on Christmas Eve.

"Proper ambrosia has only coconut and oranges in it, with homemade wine and sugar to taste," Mother would say. "Just coconut and oranges, no other additions." Our ambrosia was proper, served from a cutglass fruit bowl that stood on the sideboard the rest of the year.

Days before the ambrosia was made, I finished making my gifts: lop-sided pincushions, embroidered dresser scarfs, ribbon bookmarks with their cross-stitched monograms, tie holders fashioned of oval embroidery hoops wrapped in overlapping strips of velvet, tiny jewelry cases made of English walnut shells.

When Christmas week arrived, Omah Cleveland would drive up to the back porch with his wagon and unload our fresh cedar Christmas tree, branches of berried holly cut from the woods near his house and long strands of Southern smilax. (Years later Omah brought the smilax to decorate the church for my wedding.)

The tree was anchored in a churn in the corner of the living room near Mother's writing desk and the tall glass-front bookcases. Searchers of the Far Room were rewarded with boxes of tissue-wrapped ornaments: fragile glass birds with real feather tails, a ship with sails, bright balls, clip-on holders for candles that would be lit early Christmas morning, a star for the top that only Wilson could reach.

The smilax was draped across the brick mantel and twined around the round post that a fanciful builder had placed in the middle of the room. The holly branches were tacked over the transoms and were stuck behind pictures where they made stiff holiday backgrounds for The Angelus, Age of Innocence, and the panels of oval likenesses of English authors. Swags of smilax and clumps of holly decorated the hat rack on the hall tree and filled the jardiniere. When the tree and the smilax and the holly filled the room with the smells and colors of Christmas, Mother would walk in bearing a bowl of narcissus in full bloom.

"See?" she would say. "They did bloom for Christmas! Isn't it wonderful?"

And it was. All of it.

Depression Days

SOON AFTER ONE of those Christmases when Omah still brought our cedar tree. and our holly, when Mother's narcissus still burst into bloom to welcome the Holy Season, but when I was too old to make lumpy pincushions or to play in the fire with the poker, the security of my world began to waver.

After Christmas, during the late winter of 1933, our high school band was invited to Mobile to march in the Mardi Gras parades. We had about thirty or thirty-five members of the band, and I believe I played snare drum that year, trying to match the pace set by Preston McCreary, who could make his drum sticks fly. Preston swaggered up and down the hall at school with his drumsticks stuck in his left hip pocket where he could reach them, like a gunfighter drawing his weapon, to beat out a quick rhythm on radiators or window sills as he passed.

Tabb paid my band fee ($2.50 a month) until nepotism regulations cost her her job in the Post Office and she could no longer finance my band lessons or the rental fee on the instrument I played. I would not have been in the band during my final high school years if I had not played an instrument the band needed but which nobody would pay to play. One year I played the baritone horn, and a couple of years I played the alto.

Going to Mobile was a big adventure for most of us. We practiced marching up and down the football field and even down town and back for weeks, and we spent a lot of time learning to play while we marched. It wasn't easy.

Our uniforms were white duck pants, a red vest embellished with gold braid, a red cape lined with blue (crimson and blue were our school colors) and a stiff red and blue cap with a black patent leather bill.

"Miss Mellie" McCurdy made most of the vests and capes for the band, and they looked just as professional as uniforms made by factories. The caps were purchased from a supplier of band accessories. "Miss Mellie" lived right across the street from the school, so it was easy for us to go over for fittings or for alterations.

No members of the band had their own cars (the only student of my acquaintance who had his own car was Gerald Lowery who owned the operable motor and chassis of a Model A Ford he had assembled in his father's machine shop), so we rode to Mobile in a convoy of cars driven by the band director, his wife and our chaperones.

One or two years the band made the trip to Mobile in school trucks. Not buses. Trucks. They were homemade conveyances built to haul rural children to school, oblong wooden structures with a roof, sides about three or four feet high and long wooden benches along each side and down the middle. Roll-up curtains of heavy brown canvas kept out the cold and the rain. There was no heat. The one hundred mile trip to Mobile in a school truck took about four hours and was mighty uncomfortable, but few riders complained—we were going to Mardi Gras!

Mobile's Mardi Gras celebration, though older, is less well known than the festival in New Orleans, but we members of the Thomasville High School band, we who had never even been to New Orleans, thought Mobile's Mardi Gras was wonderful. There was not a Catholic, or even an Episcopalian, among us, so we knew nothing of the religious significance of the festival. We reveled in being out of school for three days; in watching the bright, elaborate floats with their costumed riders; in hearing spectators applaud us as we marched past; in feeding squirrels beneath the ancient oaks in Bienville Square; in riding street cars; in eating at Morrison's Cafeteria; in seeing the ships at the wharf; in meeting musicians from other high school bands—so much to crowd into such a brief time.

Huey Ford (he played trumpet in the band) took me on my

first real date during Mardi Gras, took me to the ornate Saenger Theatre to see "Flying Down To Rio." And one night Mobile police threatened to arrest some of us band members for shooting craps in the lobby of the Bienville Hotel. Mardi Gras was an exciting time.

It was late when we got back home after our 1933 trip to Mardi Gras, and I went straight to bed. Daddy came into my room early the next morning, waked me up, and asked, "Did you bring any money home from Mardi Gras?"

"Yes, sir," I said. "I brought back three or four dollars."

"That's all the money we have in the world," he said. "The bank won't open this morning. I doubt that it will ever open again."

I got out of bed, found my purse and counted into Daddy's hand the three one-dollar bills and the change I had brought back home.

"At least we can pay Thurza this week," he said.

Daddy had left the bank a few years earlier to open his own insurance agency, but what money he had was still invested in bank stock. The bank's closing made no dramatic differences in our daily lives, not right away. We had never had much money, so lack of cash was not a great shock. There was always food. Daddy's credit was good at the local grocery stores (there were no chain stores). Some farmers paid him in produce, and one failed restaurant owner settled his debt by giving Daddy gallons and gallons of AlaGa Syrup. The cans with their green and yellow labels were stacked around the baseboard of the kitchen, and we ate syrup at nearly every meal for many months.

Daddy stopped smoking cigars and changed to a cheaper brand of pipe tobacco. Mother and I sewed up the runs in our stockings and kept on wearing them. Hand-me-downs were welcome. Thurza was still in our kitchen, still took our clothes, toting them in a split oak basket atop her head, down to her house to wash. Her son, T. J., still came late every winter afternoon to fill the coal scuttles and bring in splinters (lightwood) for the fires.

Our house needed painting, but it had never been painted as

long as I could remember. The wallpaper was a little more faded and tattered. We re-read the books in our library instead of buying new ones. When time came to buy a new license plate, Daddy had to let our used Model A Ford sit in the garage for a month or two until he could get enough money for the tag.

The number of tramps coming to our back door asking for food increased, and Mother fed them all. Sometimes she brought young men in to warm by the fire while they ate, and some of them left wearing sweaters or jackets or heavy socks from her "give-away trunk" in The Far Room.

It was one of those transients who gave a name to our family's favorite breakfast dish. For Sunday morning breakfast we nearly always had baked eggs: eggs broken into a shallow, buttered baking dish with rich milk, grated cheese and dabs of butter around them. One Depression Sunday morning a tramp knocked on the kitchen door just as we were sitting down to breakfast. Mother fixed him a plate of food, including the baked eggs, and he sat on the back steps to eat.

We were busy with our Sunday morning routine, getting dressed for Sunday School, when a knock came on the back door. Mother, who responded to the knock, found our tramp guest standing on the porch with his empty plate.

"Lady," he said, "would you please give me the recipe for them eggs? They was the best I ever et!"

And thus our favorite breakfast dish received its name, Tramp Eggs.

I still earned a pass to the picture show by writing movie reviews for Cousin Earl's newspaper (actually I had been awarded a pass by the theatre manager for naming the theatre The Gem), so it did not matter that I had no spare cash for entertainment.

For years, as long as I could remember, it had been Daddy's custom to keep a little money under the brass candlestick on the mantel in his and Mother's bedroom. Dollar bills were stuffed up into the candlestick and coins were put beneath its base. When money was needed for extras—to buy a watermelon off a wagon or to pay Mr. Hinson for a basket of peaches, or to "set up" a friend to the picture show or such—the standard reply to such a request for funds was "Go look under the candlestick." Whatever money was there was for general use. After 1933 there wasn't often any money under the candlestick.

It must have been the summer of 1934 that Mother went back to college to renew her teacher's certificate. She enrolled at Montevallo for six weeks so she would be qualified to direct a program of adult education in Clarke County. My sister, Annelee, was spending her summer vacation (she was a high school English teacher in Thomasville, Georgia) in Massachusetts with her former college roommate, so I kept house for Daddy—with Thurza's help. We managed all right, Daddy and I, but we were lonesome.

Annelee had always had an unusual ability to foretell events, particularly in our family. She called it her ESP. One morning, soon after her arrival in Massachusetts, she came down to breakfast and said to her hostess,

"I had the strangest, most vivid dream last night. I saw Heddie walking across a college campus with her arms full of books. She told me, 'I've decided to go back to school. There's no need for you to cut your visit short. Kathryn will keep house while I'm away.' I can't imagine why I would have such a dream!"

In a few hours a special delivery for Annelee arrived, a letter telling her exactly what she had dreamed: Mother was returning to college and I was taking care of things at home.

It was not ESP but plain good sense that prompted Annelee to pay me a quarter for each "classic" I read the summers before I went off to college. I read nearly every book on her list except works by Dickens—she did not have enough quarters to pay me to read them!

Mother, when she returned from her schooling, set up her headquarters in the back of Daddy's insurance office. From there she directed the activities of several teachers in an early federal government program aimed at reducing adult illiteracy. She also began to learn more about the operation of an insurance agency. Hers was a part time job, and it paid very little, probably about

$40.00 a month, but it provided cash when we needed it badly. I'm sure Daddy's good friend, Dave Mathews, who was superintendent of education for the Clarke County schools, got the job for Mother as repayment for some of Daddy's past favors to him. This is not to imply that Mother was not qualified for the position. She was. And she worked diligently and effectively at it.

I remember how we all teased her when one of the first persons to register for classes was a man who said she had taught him years ago, before her marriage.

"See what you can teach Old Joe this time around!" Daddy laughed. "I'm surprised to hear he is thirsting after knowledge—I thought his thirst ran in other directions."

And Daddy told again one of his favorite tales about Joe, about how he staggered home one night, long after the midnight freight had run, drunk and thirsty, very thirsty. He drew a bucket of water from the well on his back porch and gulped down dipper after dipper of it.

The water tasted so good that Joe went in, waked up his wife and children and made them come out to drink some too, said he didn't want them to miss having anything as good as that water was!

Daddy also used to tell about one time he was going to Montgomery with Joe, going in Joe's car. Somewhere between Selma and Montgomery Joe stopped and picked up a sorry-looking, bony hound that was ambling beside the road. He put the dog in the back seat and drove on.

"Joe, why did you pick up that dog?" Daddy asked.

"Well," Joe replied, "if we found out we needed a dog, we'd have one," Joe replied.

Mother denied that Joe had ever been one of her pupils. She likely dismissed the subject by declaring "Oh tetooderly!" It was the strongest expletive she ever used.

I don't remember now how long Mother worked with the adult education program. Maybe a year or two. Maybe longer. I do know that she devoted more and more time to the insurance agency as Daddy's health began to fail.

Daddy lost weight and tired easily. Dr. Irons said his heart was weak, that he needed rest, needed more than just the short nap he had taken after dinner (midday) for years. Daddy said what he needed was turnip greens and pot likker with Thurza's cornbread crumbled up in it. He didn't seem sick, just weary. He went to the office every day, but Mother gradually took over the routine tasks, renewing policies and sending out statements and such. I helped in the office, too.

Daddy was in the audience, along with Mother and Aunt Bet and Tabb, when I and the thirty-two other members of the Class of 1935 graduated from Thomasville High School. He approved of the welcome address I, as class president, gave. "Keep it short," he had told me. I did.

We had no caps and gowns that depression-time graduation, no annual. For our senior trip we rode a school truck to Beck's Landing on the Alabama River, about twenty miles away, where we camped out (well chaperoned) overnight. Some class members set out trot lines and fished all night. A few played cards. I suppose the wildest thing that went on that night was some of us girls smoking cigarettes. Mine was an Old Gold.

There were some parties for the graduates, a tea or two for the girls, and a couple of picnics at Bradford's Pond. The most humorous event, the one added to our serigamy of stories, occurred at our baccalaureate sermon when Tabb fell off the stage. The service was held in the high school auditorium, and the joint choirs from the Methodist and Baptist churches sang. The choir members were all seated on the stage. After we graduates had marched in and had taken our places on the front rows (the reserved seats were marked with roses, our class flower), the choir stood for their opening anthem. Somehow Cousin Tabb got the heel of her shoe caught in the rounds of her chair, and she plunged off the stage. She was not hurt, did not even tear her stockings. In fact, she regained her composure enough to take her place in the choir again.

My friend Ruth and I never regained our composure. We giggled, as decorously as possible, throughout the rest of the service. So did Tabb—every time she looked at us. We laughed about "Tabb's tumble" all summer.

During that summer I tried to finish reading the books on Annelee's list (except for Dickens), played tennis on the court we built in Clay Park (most of us had broken strings in our tennis rackets, and the few balls we had were all dead—some days we couldn't even get up enough money to buy lime to line the court), swam occasionally at Bradford's Pond, got together with friends, helped in the office. Then when the spider lilies were blooming by the front steps and the scuppernongs on the arbor by the chicken house were ripe, it was time to go to college.

I was awarded a small scholarship to Huntingdon College in Montgomery, and I also had an NYA work scholarship (I was assigned to be an assistant in the biology-zoology lab—I who had never been in a lab), so I could afford to enter college. Since Mother and my two sisters had graduated from Huntingdon when it was Woman's College of Alabama, it was natural that I, too, should go there.

I packed my belongings in a green steamer trunk Daddy had won as a premium for selling insurance, and boarded the train for Montgomery.

I did well in my studies (my placement exams put me in Dr. Rhoda Ellison's English class where she encouraged me to write about my small town background), all except French. My schooling had left me totally unprepared to learn a foreign language.

The first grading period, I failed French. It was the first F I had ever gotten, and I thought the world had ended. So far as I knew, nobody in my family had ever failed anything. I was humiliated, ashamed, sure I had disgraced my family. I was particularly worried about what Daddy's reaction would be to that F in French. To make matters worse, I was going home for the first time the weekend after those grades were mailed. The timing was terrible.

When I got off the train in Thomasville, Daddy wasn't there, but everybody else was glad to see me. They didn't act as if I had ruined the family name. Nobody mentioned grades. We walked up the hill to the house, and I saw an envelope from Huntingdon

College on the brick mantel in the living room. It had been opened. Still nobody mentioned grades.

Daddy got home, and he was affectionate and loving, said he was happy I had come home. But he said nothing about my grades. All during supper, there was no mention of grades. The longer the topic was postponed, the more uncomfortable and apprehensive I became.

After supper we moved into the living room. I saw Daddy look up at that envelope on the mantel. I wanted to hide. I felt worse than I used to feel before one of Cousin Golda's piano recitals.

Daddy filled his pipe and got it lighted before he said anything. After he leaned back in his chair, he said, "Well, I've been to Grove Hill and Jackson and Walker Springs and Whatley and Gosport today. And everywhere I went, people were speaking English."

That's all he ever said about my French grade. I passed the course the next grading period.

At the end of my freshman year, when I came home for summer vacation, Daddy was sick, bedridden by what was termed "failing health." Mother's letters to me had told of his illness, but she, being of both an optimistic and protective nature, had not prepared me for the seriousness, the finality, of his ailment.

I don't recall that anyone ever told me exactly what was the matter with Daddy, but, looking back, I believe he suffered from congestive heart failure compounded by other health problems. Dr. Irons stopped by to see him nearly every day that summer, and Mr. Luther Moore came about once a week to shave Daddy and to trim his hair.

"I couldn't holler, 'Sooey!' if the hogs had me," Daddy would say to visitors who asked how he felt. Not once during that summer did he feel well enough to come out on the porch to rock and tell tales. The chairs (there were no new covers for the cushions that year) sat empty—and lonesome.

Even as his strength ebbed away, Daddy remained concerned about his insurance agency. Each day he gave Mother and me instructions about renewing policies, soliciting new business and collecting old accounts. Several times we had to bring the account books home for him to go over, almost as if to verify the accuracy of the figures he carried in his head. We read the business mail to him, and he dictated replies.

Mother and I took turns staying in the insurance office. Annelee, her school-teaching year ended, was there to help at home. Aunt Bet and Tabb were in and out of his sick room several times daily, bringing news of the happenings downtown. Thurza, blessed Thurza, kept his room clean, washed his sheets and pillow cases in the tubs in her back yard and ironed them with flat irons heated in her open fireplace, and used her skill as a cook to tempt "Mr. Jim's" appetite. It was also Thurza who stood by his bed and fanned him with a palmetto fan when the oppressive heat of summer afternoons made his breathing difficult. We all took turns fanning.

On those hot afternoons I fixed big glasses of lemonade for Daddy, making them just the way I made his "after nap" treats on Sunday afternoons when I was growing up. Daddy used to brag on my lemonades; said nobody, not even the folks at Peoples Drug Store, could make them as good as mine.

Daddy lapsed into a coma during the final days of his illness. He roused occasionally, and twice he asked for me, but each time I was away from the house, and he slipped into unconsciousness again before I returned. So I never knew what he wanted to tell me.

Sometimes when I went into his room during those periods when he was unaware of anyone's presence or identity, I would find him moving his right hand in the air as though he were writing down and adding columns of figures, perhaps trying to balance a ledger sheet. Even when I spoke to him, he continued his troubled efforts to cope with his invisible financial problems.

Daddy died in August, just before his seventieth birthday. Dr. Irons was with him (he had spent the night on the leather couch in the living room, just outside Daddy's door), and Mother sat beside him, holding his hand and repeating the Twenty-third Psalm.

We had his funeral services at home the next day. His coffin was in the living room, in front of the bookcases filled with the books he had collected. Friends crowded into that living room and onto the porches and overflowed into the yard, the sidewalk and the street. They stood silently while his minister read the Methodist ritual for the burial of the dead. His brothers served as pallbearers.

That night, the night after his funeral, Mother slept in Daddy's bed, the bed where he had died, and I lay beside her that long, hot night.

In a few weeks I returned to Montgomery for my sophomore year at Huntingdon. When I came home for Thanksgiving holidays, the mortgage on our house had been foreclosed, most of our furniture had been sold, and Mother was living with Aunt Bet and Tabb. Mother's writing desk was saved from the sale of property as were the tall, glass-front bookcases with their treasures of books, six hand-crafted chairs that had come with the Tabb family from Virginia, and the small, walnut, drop-leaf table that stood beside Daddy's bed to hold his pipe, matches and tobacco. Although his smoking paraphernalia had long since been discarded, for almost a quarter of a century after his death the odor of tobacco clung to those drawers, and each time I opened them, I almost felt his presence.

I never knew what became of the halltree or the heavy dining room table with its handcarved dragon pedestals or the sideboard with its beveled mirror and its long drawers that held table cloths and monogrammed napkins and its deep recesses where Mother's Christmas narcissus bowls were sometimes hiding. Those are the pieces I miss most.

Our old house was vacant for a while. Then one day when I walked past on my way to town, I saw a new family sitting on the front porch, rocking and telling a serigamy of stories of their own.